DARK PSYCHOLOGY

AND MANIPULATION

How to change your life drastically influencing anyone with the Powerful strategic techniques of Dark psychology and Manipulation, Brainwashing, NLP secret and science of Persuasion and Hypnosis.

KNIGHT PSYCHE

circumstances will any legal responsibility or blame be held against the publisher for any reparation, damages, or monetary loss due to the information herein, either directly or indirectly.

Respective authors own all copyrights not held by the publisher.

The information herein is offered for informational purposes solely and is universal as such. The presentation of the information is without a contract or any type of guarantee assurance.

The trademarks that are used are without any consent, and the publication of the trademark is without permission or backing by the trademark owner. All trademarks and brands within this book are for clarifying purposes only and are owned by the owners themselves, not affiliated with this document.

Contents

Introduction 8

Chapter 1: Dark Psychology – The Fundamentals 10

   1.1.   Traits of dark psychology...14
      a.   Narcissism 16
      b.   Machiavellianism...18
      c.   Psychopathy 21
      d.   Sadism...23

Chapter 2: Elements of Dark Psychology............................27

   2.1. Deception 28

   2.2. Manipulation..29

   2.3. Covert Emotional Manipulation 30

   2.4. Persuasion..30

   2.5. Hypnosis 31

   2.6. Brainwashing 32

Chapter 3: Understanding Deception 33

   3.1. What is Deception?..33

   3.2. Types of Deception 35
      a.   Concealments 35
      b.   Exaggeration..36
      c.   Lies...36
      d.   Equivocations...37
      e.   Understatements 37

   3.3. Components of Deception.......................................37
      a.   Disguise 38
      b.   Camouflage...39
      c.   Simulation 39

   3.4. Detecting Deception...40

Chapter 4: Manipulation and Techniques of Manipulation...............44

   4.1. Definition of Manipulation 45

4.2. Techniques of Manipulation...47
   A.   Gaslight..47
   B.   Projection...48
   C.   Isolation...49
   D.   Positive Reinforcement 50
   E.   Negative reinforcement 51
   F.   Punishment 52
   G.   Nagging...52
   H.   Yelling..53
   I.   Silent treatment..54
   J.   Intimidation...55
   K.   Traumatic One trial learning 57
   L.   Manipulation of facts 57
   M.   Creating an illusion 59
   N.   Putting others down 59
   O.   Leading questions 60

4.3. Behavioral Traits Of The Manipulator 61
   A.   Deception through lying....................................62
   B.   Lying by omission 63
   C.   Denial..63
   D.   Avoidance...64
   E.   Rationalization 65
   F.   Playing victims..65
   G.   Generate fear...66
   H.   Create Insecurity 66

4.4. Recognition Of The Toxic Relationship..67

4.5. Prevention From Being Manipulated 68

4.6. Selection Of Favorite Victim For Manipulators.........................69
   A.   Emotional Insecure 70
   B.   Sensitive People 70
   C.   Empathic People 70
   D.   Fear of Loneliness...71
   E.   Personality Dependent Disorder 71

Chapter 5: Covert Emotional Manipulation 72

5.1. Definition of Covert Emotional Manipulation...........................72

5.2. Techniques Of Covert Emotional Manipulation 74
   A.   Emotional intimidation 74
   B.   Triangulation...75
   C.   The blame games..77
   D.   The bait and switch 77

E.   The law of state transference 78
F.   Leading Questions...78
G.   Insinuation..79

Chapter 6: Persuasion and Its Methods................................81

6.1. Definition of persuasion...82

6.2. Methods of persuasion 83
A.   Ethos...84
B.   Pathos 85
C.   Logos...85

6.3. Techniques of Persuasion 87
A.   The door in the face...88
B.   Foot in the door 88
C.   Yes- set trick...89
D.   Linguistic presupposition....................................90
E.   Reverse psychology 90
F.   Blackmail 91
G.   Love bombing..92
H.   Positive reinforcement 93

6.4. Empathy and Persuasion..93

6.5. How To Influence & Persuade?...............................94

6.7. Persuasion Techniques In Business.........................96

6.8. Persuasion by mass media and advertisement........98

6.9. Persuasion in intimate relations............................101

Chapter 7: Hypnosis, Its Types, and Uses 104

7.1. Definition of Hypnosis 104

7.2. Types of Hypnosis..106

7.3. Uses Of Hypnosis 110

7.4. Neuro -Linguistic Programming..............................113
7.4.1. Types of Neuro-Linguistic Programming 114

7.5. Mechanism of Neuro-Linguistic Programming........117

7.6. Different Types of Communications.........................120
7.6.1. Verbal communications...................................121
7.6.2. Types of Verbal Communication 121
7.6.3. Non- Verbal Communication 123
7.6.4. Types of non-verbal communication 123

7.7. Improvement in body language *127*

Chapter 8. The Technique of Brainwashing **131**

8.1. Definition of Brainwashing *131*

8.2. Steps of Brainwashing *132*

8.3. Techniques of Brainwashing *137*

8.4. Prevention from Brainwashing *145*

Conclusion **149**

Introduction

What exactly does psychology imply? As the study of the soul, psychology can be portrayed as having its beginning and end with the mind due to the wonderful brains that have come before us. It isn't all science, though, since it includes conscious and unconscious components. It also includes behavioral habits. Many people have found human brains to be perplexing and fascinating. As a result, they have pursued careers in psychology, experimental research, and philosophy to unravel this mystery: the human brain. They are responsive and assisting people in dealing with issues such as anxiety and depression. With their help, our pain is suppressed, and we are free to live our lives.

In neuropsychology, a field of psychology concerned with the relationship between the brain and behavior and emotions, the aim is to understand the human psyche. How do the brains gather information? What method is used to process this data? Finally, where do you put the information? These problems have to do with neuropsychology. Identifying how well the mind works entails more than just seeing a psychiatrist for advice and medication or just a thorough grasp of the brain. It goes a lot further. It would go much deeper. It is both good and evil in each of us. As per Colin McGinn, bad people love distress in particular and vise - versa. Humans have all of these emotions: anxiety, pleasure, excitement, pain, and grief, and we can also hurt others due to our inability to control our emotional reactions. For several years, people have been intrigued by the concept of mind control. The newspapers and movies have told stories of communities of brainwashed or hypnotized people into doing acts they would not have done otherwise. There have been individuals across both ends of the discussion others agree that mind control does not exist, so it is just a hoax, while some claim that they might be controlled at any time by mind domination. This handbook explains some of the various kinds of mind manipulation, how they function, and whether they can be used in everyday life.

Chapter 1: Dark Psychology – The Fundamentals

Now read carefully what I have written for you because it is very powerful information that can change your life. Dark psychology involves the science of how we consciously and purposefully harm people. Mind domination and deception are at the heart of dark psychology. As human beings, it is often stated that we all seem to have a "darkness inside." According to Christian beliefs, man has an inherent sin or evil. The darkness inside us will also lead us to do something surprising. For instance, take an individual: you figured they were nice, but then they do something unpredictable one day, and we no longer want to communicate with them.

Dark psychology is concerned with mind control and coercion. This craft of manipulating and convincing someone to do your bidding starts with a child screaming for their parents to come to their aid at a young age. It is replicated each time the child expresses an interest in something. Parents may consider this to be innocent, and no parent wishes to see their child cry. Parents who may not intervene ensure that their children are subjected to manipulation later in life. It's just about esoteric psychology. Gain insight into a person's thoughts and patterns of behavior. Let us now attempt to acquaint ourselves with the numerous effects of dark psychology, having explained this otherwise broad subject. Dark psychology has an impact on both the perpetrator and the victim. People who belong to the Dark Triad are prone to wearing two masks. It is a phenomenon that has been seen in many Dark Psychology theories. Someone you don't like on your squad is acting to be someone else to gain attention, authority, and influence. When interacting with strangers, you must tread cautiously and be aware of red signs that will save you from being involved with a negative personality. It's important to keep yourself safe from predators such as Adolf Hitler and Jim Jones. Of necessity, these are serious examples. Many individuals have people in their lives or quite dear to them with strikingly identical characteristics to these two guys. Recognizing them will help you improve both your mental health and your wellbeing.

You may have seen or read references to "a shadow inside" in films or novels. It has been mentioned by some of the world's most illustrious thinkers. The Christians' holy book describes how "man's heart is sinful." We've all seen the one person who seems to be unusually quiet or cautious in social situations, just for the same person to commit a duplicitous act that makes it impossible to equate the act with the person in question. Often, we are that person. It is not wholly surprising, as shocking as it might be. Those are induced reactions to external circumstances. The pot was mixed, and the dark feelings that had been simmering under the surface bubbled to the top. When dominance is gained, they typically fade away. When the correct "buttons" are pressed, everybody has a latent propensity to be a little naughty or sometimes outright cruel. Others, on the other hand, have complete control of their dark feelings. They raise them, feed them, and then when it suits their needs, they deliberately release them to the detriment of everyone else.

These feelings are often cultivated from a young age. When an infant scream in a particular manner, the people in their life hurry to do what they want. If the parents do not teach their children early on that this is false, they will grow up believing the others in their lives can be exploited to do their will. As they get older, they will stop crying as a tool, but they will continue to manipulate others. They use impulses other than tears to threaten their victims. As a result, what began as a harmless childish activity has evolved into a dark desire for power. The extent to which this person would go to assert power would determine the severity of their acts. The analysis of a person's thought process is what dark psychology is all about. It aims to uncover the motivation underlying these actions and the trends that emerge from before to after they are committed to shedding some light on how an individual can willingly see these actions through completion while being aware of the potential for harm and pain to others. The sinister side of human personality is illuminated by dark psychology.

1.1. Traits of dark psychology

The "dark triad," which comprises three negative behavioral characteristics, narcissism, Machiavellianism, and psychopathy, has been alluded to by psychologists for a long time. However, several researchers in the area have recently argued that commonplace sadism should be included in the catalog of big dark psychological characteristics. As a result, we've shifted our focus away from the negative triumvirate but toward the "four dark psychology characteristics." We'll focus on each of the four characteristics in this section and go through them in depth. Once we get at those characteristics, it's important to remember that knowing them is essential if you'd like to know how to prevent being fooled. Indeed, research into these characteristics has a wide range of uses, from clinical psychologists, law enforcement, and even company management.

According to studies, individuals who rank high on the four characteristics are more likely to commit crimes, cause trouble within institutions, pose harm to the people in their life, and bring pain to society as a whole. It could be necessary to hold individuals with those characteristics out of positions of authority in the workplace. We are constantly exposed to narcissism, Machiavellianism, sadism, and psychopathy, and if we are vigilant, we will be able to detect them. We always have these characteristics to some degree, according to statistics. In reality, psychologists use research approaches that suggest certain characteristics appear on a continuum as they assess individuals for them. For instance, instead of seeing those that are sadistic and others who are not sadistic, certain studies indicate that we have individuals that have elevated amounts of sadism and others that have low concentrations of sadism.

Another factor to keep in mind is that most of the behaviors shared by individuals with one of the four traits will differ, which can be confounding, particularly for those with formal psychology experience. Narcissists, for example, can act in ways comparable to Machiavellians or sadists. As a result, simply watching someone for a brief amount of time might not be enough to determine what sort of dark characteristic they possess. If anyone does something harmful to others, you may be able to figure out which dark attribute they have by looking at their motive or the scope of their evil deed. Don't leap to conclusions; instead, take your time to observe the person's behavior before passing judgment carefully. It can be difficult to be rational when evaluating a person's dark personality attribute if the person's behaviors are harmful to you. Hence, it's vital to note that you can only work with people properly if you have a solid knowledge of certain characteristics and motives. It would help if you attempted to distance yourself from the scenario and evaluate the individual from the perspective of a neutral third party.

a. Narcissism

People that are narcissists exhibit a black characteristic known as narcissism. Egomania, arrogance, domination, and entitlement are all characteristics of narcissists. Narcissists are beautiful people with an optimistic attitude, which is how they're so successful at deceiving others. As per psychiatrists, narcissists are typically on the hunt for individuals who can tap into their "narcissistic source" to support their egos. They are also incapable of compassion for others. One of the most common characteristics of narcissists is their ability to create and cultivate relationships. They may initially blind others to the possibility that they are behaving in their self-interest. We may have narcissistic characteristics to some degree, but only a handful of us develop Narcissistic Personality

Disorder Narcissus, a Greek mythological figure, inspired the words narcissist and narcissism. Narcissus had been a hunter who became very beautiful. Everybody seems to form a relationship with him because he was so attractive.

On the other hand, he only treated others with scorn and disrespect and never returned others' affection. As a result, Nemesis (the goddess of vengeance) cursed him to come crashing in love with his projection in a puddle of water.

Modern-day narcissists, like Narcissus, are enamored of themselves. However, researchers have discovered that narcissists are obsessed with perfect representations of themselves that only live in their fantasies, not with actual versions of themselves. It's tempting to believe that narcissists have elevated self-esteem, but this isn't the case; they have a twisted sort of self-esteem based on enjoying a fictitious grandiloquent version rather than embracing or loving themselves. When a narcissist behaves with self-interest to the detriment of others, it's normally in the service of the grand image of himself, although he admits it's not true. The self-importance of narcissists is underestimated. They believe they are entitled to be handled differently than anyone else. They have an inflated sense of superiority, believing that it is for the greater good when they are treated well in such cases. When a narcissist takes full benefit of you, he believes he is doing you a favor. He will rationalize a lot of greed and bad behavior this way. A narcissist would believe that he is more valuable and worthy than another person in a relationship. A narcissist in the workplace would believe that he has more innate talent than his coworkers and, as a result, needs to be in charge of tasks or rewarded ahead of anyone else. The fascinating aspect regarding narcissism is that it can also lead to prosperity. Narcissism has the potential to become a self-fulfilling prophecy. When a narcissist thinks he is better than anyone else, he will put in extra effort to justify it, and as a result, he will be more successful in his profession. When a narcissist feels he wants to be in a leadership position, he will exude optimism and develop leadership qualities, and those around him will believe he needs to be their leader.

b. Machiavellianism

Machiavellianism is a darker personality disorder characterized by deception and coercion. Machiavellians are pessimistic by nature (not because they are cynical or curious; they do not value the normative constraints that most humans comply with).

They are usually unethical and self-serving. They may not have an understanding of; righteousness and erroneous they'll do whatever they can as much as it suits them. Machiavellians are harsh, irresponsible, and inherently skilled at manipulating others. They assume that everything is a negligible game and that exploiting others is the secret to survival. They treat all sorts of affairs with a cynical, calculated mentality, and the end often excuses the means to them because they want a certain result in a particular situation. Niccolò Machiavelli, an Italian political philosopher best known for his book The Prince, is the inventor of Machiavellianism. The book guides how to influence and dominate the crowds in terms of achieving authority over them. People are taught through this book to be sly, dishonest, and deceptive as far as they obtain what they need. It claims that harming others is ethically correct in the service of one's desires. In this way, Machiavellianism and narcissism are identical in that each has an overarching conviction that an individual's desires represent the general good, although it means harming others. People with these characteristics are more likely to steal, lie, and hurt others to accomplish their goals. They are emotionally disconnected from others surrounding them; therefore, you will find that all of your impressions are superficial when you're in a relationship with them. They would not be reluctant to hurt anyone if it is in their best interests. Whereas psychopaths, narcissists, and sadists can hurt others for their pleasure, absence of empathy, as well as to satisfy those needs and wants, Machiavellians would do it for a reasonable and potentially logical reason. They don't give a damn about the emotional harm they cause; in truth, they just care about other people's feelings if they realize it will end up hurting them.

In contrast to "hot empathy," Machiavellians appear to have "cold empathy." Cold empathy is the ability to understand how people might behave or respond in specific circumstances or how things might occur. On the opposite hand, hot empathy leads to being mindful of and thinking for the feelings of someone in a particular scenario. Normal human beings possess hot empathy, which ensures they appreciate how others feel and try not to offend those around them. Machiavellians are good at predicting what someone will do in a given situation, but they aren't good at recognizing other's feelings.

As a consequence, they come off as unapproachable, socially detached, and aggressive. Machiavellians are master manipulators who are prone to white-collar crime. Embezzlement schemes, pyramid schemes, stock swindling schemes, overpricing schemes, and political offenses are common among people who have this tendency. They exploit people to reach the top, and as they reach powerful positions (either in business or politics), they often use the same tactics to control the public.

c. Psychopathy

Psychopathy is by far the most malicious of all the dark qualities. Psychopaths show a poor degree of sensitivity and are unconcerned with others. They, on the other hand, are reckless and thrill-seeking people with extraordinarily high levels of hyperactivity. They are spiteful, manipulative, and have an exaggerated sense of self-importance. They are only interested in exhilaration and are unconcerned with the hurt they do to others. Psychopaths are harder to detect than you would expect. They strive to maintain regular physical appearances; through their lack of empathy and morality, they learn to behave naturally by watching the emotional responses of others. When they're trying to trick you, they can even appear appealing. They are erratic, and some have violent behavior, although this is not necessarily the case.

Psychopaths arouse a lot of curiosity and fascination,

which explains why there are so many examples in popular culture. Fascination, on the other hand, brings with it a slew of myths. We prefer to image psychopaths as serial murderers, bombers, super villains, and individuals that are clinically psychotic. Still, the risk is that we ignore that most psychopaths are simply ordinary people who can hurt us in other ways. Psychopaths like fighting battles, disregarding others' feelings and lying to you regularly.

Adult psychopathy is incurable. Once psychopathic traits are discovered in adolescents and teenagers, they should be taught to become slightly cynical and more courteous towards others by specific programs. The distinction between a sociopath and a psychopath is crucial to comprehend. These two words are frequently used synonymously in everyday conversations, but they have distinct meanings in psychology. A sociopath is an individual with antisocial characteristics. Now, antisocial traits are typically the consequence of environmental and social factors. For instance, a person who had a traumatic upbringing may develop out to be a sociopath because he distrusts society in general or has acquired such psychiatric problems due to his upbringing. Psychopathic traits, on the opposite hand, are inherited. Psychopaths are not created; they are birthed, psychopaths. On the other hand, social and environmental influences can play a role in a person's specific form of psychopathy. Individuals born with psychopathic tendencies and raised in a dysfunctional and aggressive environment, for instance, are much more inclined to have more severe signs of their psychopathy. According to experts, genetics, brain structure, and environmental causes are also thought to play a role in psychopathy.

Psychopathy, as the other dark characteristics, is a continuum. Physicians use a scale rating method to determine the severity of psychopathy; anyone falls anywhere on the scale, but those with a ranking of 30 or higher are known to have clinically relevant psychopathy.

d. Sadism

Sadism is marked as callousness, much as those three dark characteristics.

Sadists have normal degrees of impulsivity and coercion, which is why they weren't initially included in the "dark triad." Sadists are described by their desire to inflict suffering on others.

From all appearances, everyday sadists are mild and

functioning people who love hurting others. Sadists are tended to as "everyday sadists," and it's necessary to distinguish them from narcissists, Machiavellians, and psychopaths that can show sadism as part of their other dark characteristics. Perhaps if they are truly innocent, sadists are inherently willing to hurt others. Sadists can prioritize the alleviation of physical distress on others, even though it occurs at a personal cost Violence is pleasurable and thrilling to them, and it can also be sexually satisfying. Sadists are often attracted to careers that encourage them to hurt others while seeming to be doing real work. As a result, many gravitate toward police departments, the military, and other related fields. When the rates of sadism in law enforcement are related to the rates of sadism in the regular populace, psychologists have found that the levels of police departments are often higher. This may understand how some police officers had issues with some other members from taking the law into their own hands.

Sadists have a penchant for inflicting suffering on those surrounding them for no purpose. They are likely to intensify if they notice that the individual in question becomes least likely to resist. This illustrates why abusers continue to target those who refuse to face up to them.

Sadists are the type of individuals who would reveal them to others after pledging to keep your secrets private because they love it when you are in distress. They are much more likely to represent people in misleading or unflattering words to damage the other person's credibility.

In contrast, Machiavellians may perform this to further their agenda; sadists do so because it is enjoyable. Sadists can also deliberately work to make you terminated from the job or negatively affect your success, not to gain an advantage over you, but just to make you miserable. They can even threaten to destroy your relationships by causing strife in your relationship and then sitting back and enjoying the drama and suffering. They are most likely to rob other people's goods as they don't like the other people to get them, not that they require it. They are most prone to threaten you in person or on the internet. A sadist will still be identified by his online messages and remarks. The majority of internet trolls are regular sadists. They can make sarcastic remarks on almost anything to offend you or bring a response out of you, not as they believe in their own opinion, simply they wish to bother you or bring a reaction out of you. Sometimes the most cohesive things online can still elicit a hostile response. The more you interact with bullies, the more energized they get and the further they can annoy you online.

Chapter 2: Elements of Dark Psychology

The concept of mind control exists around for quite some time. People have been fascinated by and terrified by the prospect of someone being able to manipulate their minds and force them to do something beyond their consent. According to conspiracy theories, political leaders and other powerful figures are accused of using their abilities to manipulate what small numbers of people do. And in criminal trials, the defense of brainwashing has been used to explain why people committed the crimes they are guilty of. Despite the media's and movies' dramatic portrayals of mind control, little is learned about the many forms of brain control and how they function. As an intro to understanding this fascinating subject, this chapter will look at some of the most popular elements of mind control. Although several different forms of brain control can manipulate the alleged target, the six most common ones are listed below. Brainwashing, covert emotional manipulation, hypnosis, manipulation, persuasion, and deception are among them. All of these will be covered further down.

2.1. Deception

The idea of deception is one that often appears in the realm of dark psychology. It has been described over time as any action performed by a dishonest person to reinforce in the victim certain convictions that are typically false or only partially true. It is also grouped with deception, mystification, and suffrage. Deception is a difficult concept to grasp because it encompasses too many distinct elements, such as distractions, propaganda camouflage, and concealment. Since the target often leads to enormous confidence in this dishonest figure, the manipulator can also effortlessly dominate the victim's mind. The victims frequently accept whatever the manipulator says, and they can also design their futures and shape their life around what the manipulator feeds their subconscious mind. Once the victim understands what is going on, this powerful aspect of confidence in the manipulator will easily vanish. Because of this, a certain amount of expertise is required to execute this motif, as just then will a trickster be enabled to deftly shift the subject of doubt away from himself and into the victim's fear.

2.2. Manipulation

Manipulation is a form of mind control that might be applied in various ways to influence how a person thinks. Manipulation will be used to connect to psychological manipulation in this book. This is a form of social control that aims to alter other people's actions or perceptions. It is accomplished by the use of abusive, manipulative, and underhanded methods. This type of mind control is being used to further the manipulator's desires to the detriment of others. The techniques used are often described as manipulative, devious, violent, and exploitative. Many people are aware that they are being controlled and when those surrounding them are becoming manipulated, but they are unaware that this is brain control. Since the coercion normally occurs among the target and anyone they trust well, this may be a complicated means of brain control to prevent.

2.3. Covert Emotional Manipulation

People who wish to exert influence or authority over you use misleading and underhanded strategies to manipulate your emotions covertly. People like this try to alter the manner you perceive and act without you even noticing it. To put it another way, they use tactics to manipulate your beliefs so that you believe you are acting on your inner free choice. Covert emotional coercion is the so-called that it operates without you being mindful of it. People who are skilled at using those tactics can manipulate you into doing their business despite your understanding; they can "psychologically enslave" you.

2.4. Persuasion

Persuasion is a dark psychology theme that has a lot in common with deception. This is because they are both used to manipulate a victim's motivations, behaviors, emotions, and values. There are various explanations why we use persuasion in our daily lives, but the most important is to bring people from opposing viewpoints together. For example, in the workplace, the persuasive approach would be applied to change a person's attitude toward a product, an idea, or a current situation. Through the procedure, typed or spoken sentences convey the other person's thoughts, feelings, or details. Another typical use of persuasion is to achieve a personal advantage. It may mean advocating for a trial as part of a promotional advertisement or during a political campaign. And the fact that none of them are considered positive or bad, they are all used to persuade the listener to act or affirm somehow.

2.5. Hypnosis

Many people have attempted to define hypnosis. The American Psychological Association defines hypnosis as a reciprocal relationship in which the hypnotist makes recommendations to the subject and chooses which ones he or she may answer to. If somebody is hypnotized, Edmonton claims that they are simply in a profound mental state. As a result, hypnosis occurs when a person reaches a mental state in which he or she is responsive to the ideas of a hypnotist. Many people have witnessed hypnosis in movies, cartoons, or at magic shows or concerts where performers are instructed to do routine acts and then do so. One thing is certain: many people believe in hypnosis and will go to great lengths to prevent being a survivor, while others believe it is a work of fiction.

2.6. Brainwashing

The basic method of mind control to examine is brainwashing. Brainwashing is the act of convincing others to reject previous convictions in favor of new ideas and values. There are many approaches to do this, but not each of them is undesirable. When you are born in

Africa and migrate to America, you will frequently be compelled to modify your beliefs and expectations in an attempt to settle in with the unfamiliar society and environment. Those in slave camps, on the other hand, or where a new dictator regime takes over, will always go through a brainwashing procedure to get people to obey along peacefully.

Click here if you want to know the TEN STRATEGIC AND POWERFUL SALES PERSUASION TECHNIQUES for Free →
http://bit.ly/10strategic

Chapter 3: Understanding Deception

The basic type of mind control is deception. Let's take a detailed look.

3.1. What is Deception?

To begin, a concept of deception is necessary. Deception, including deceit, falseness, hoax, subterfuge, and managerial behavior, is a technique used by the perpetrator to get the target to believe facts that are false or only partially true. Concealment, disguise, diversion, sleight of hands, disinformation, and dissimulation are only a few examples of deception. Since the subject will believe the agent, the agent would be free to monitor the subject's mind. The target will trust what the agent said, and they will also build plans for the future and construct their world around what the agent has instructed them. The things the agent has been saying the target are wrong when the agent is using deceit. If the subject figures out, trust will potentially be lost. Hence the investigator must be skilled at lying and adept at flipping things around to keep working with their target. Deception is often encountered in couples, leading to mistrust and betrayal among the two people involved. It is because deceit goes against the laws of most marriages and is thought to get a detrimental effect on the relationship's aspirations. Most people need to be prepared to have an honest dialogue with their mate; but, once they discover that the partner is deceitful, they must learn how to use Deception and Deception to obtain the accurate and truthful facts they require. The partnership's confidence will be lost as well, making it impossible to restore the relationship to its former state. The target would constantly doubt the agent's statements, unsure whether the claim was real or fabricated. Because of this new distrust, most relationships will fail if the subject discovers the agent's deceit.

3.2. Types of Deception

As previously said, this type of communication relies on lies and omissions to get the victim to believe whatever the manipulative person leads him to believe. Given this, there are five major forms of deception techniques that have been identified. To best understand this theme, we'll go over each one quickly.

a. Concealments

Concealment is where the dishonest person intentionally omits material from his tales that are always true and valuable to the context. It is perhaps the most widely practiced method of deceit.

They may also partake in such behaviors that indicate the

concealment of pertinent knowledge to the target at the moment. A professional manipulator is wise enough to recognize that it is safer not to be blunt with their method but then to assert the deception, driving the target to their certain predicted outcome

b. Exaggeration

What can be done in response to this? It is where a person, in a way, exaggerates the facts to steer the narrative in the course that determines the optimal. To stop lying outright to their victims, the trickster will make a situation sound more serious than it is. It is typically intended to allow the perpetrator to do anything they wish.

c. Lies

It is a strategy that we as individuals employed regularly for various reasons. We are frequently tempted to lie to escape any kind of punishment.

For instance, if you serve in a bank and are late due to a small issue, you might feel allowed to comment to your employer to avoid being laid off. But what is the significance of this? It is where someone offers details that are far from the facts. They will confuse the victim with fully false evidence so that they will consider it.

d. Equivocations

A person makes a comment that is contrary to the dictionary meaning to drive the victim down a road of doubt over what is going on. It is normally a devious strategy that allows the trickster to retain his picture if he is ultimately exposed.

e. Understatements

It occurs when an individual minimizes facets of the facts of the narrative that is being shared at the moment. They may sometimes confront a survivor to demonstrate that this isn't such a big issue when, in truth, it is critical.

What motivates a trickster to use the dark psychology theme? According to studies conducted, there are typically three major factors that drive someone to deceive others over the years. Close partnerships are the general concept for all three reasons. Self-focused motivations, relationship-focused motives, and partner-focused motives are among them.

3.3. Components of Deception

Although it can be impossible to pinpoint which variables demonstrate deceit, certain subtle elements serve as instant markers of these concepts. Once the trickster delivers a blatant deception, can the survivor become mindful of these causes? Now let us delve into the specifics of the elements in question.

a. Disguise

The first element we'll dissect would be that of disguises. What generally happens has been that the trickster works long and hard before he succeeds in giving the appearance of being something he is not. Tricksters also use this strategy because they try to bury something for themselves so deeply that no one notices. It could be a hidden secret or something as innocuous as a person's name. This element's common perception is that it is just a change of clothing, as in the movies, but it is far more than that, as it often entails a radical shift in identity. Now that you have a basic understanding of what discusses work, let's look at some explanations of where they might be used in deceit.

The first is when the manipulator disguises himself as someone else to avoid being discovered. An outsider would undertake it to re-enter perhaps a group of people who dislike him, overhaul their entire identity to have others like them, or even achieve their specific personal interests.

b. Camouflage

It is where a person works diligently to conceal the reality in some manner, leaving his victim completely unaware of what is happening.

It is distinguished by the manipulator's utilization of half-truths when disclosing facts to his target. When the facts are revealed, the survivor may only be conscious that camouflage has occurred.

A professional trickster with a great deal of experience with disguise is more likely to go undetected when doing these acts.

c. Simulation

The third element of deceit is what is generally known as simulation. It is essentially the act of repeatedly showing the survivor content matter that is completely inaccurate in any way. A little further, we learn that simulation is made up of three different methods. They are impersonation, deception, and fabrication.

Fabrication is when a trickster brings something that exists in the real world and cringes it into something entirely new.

The manipulator will attempt to either detail incidents that never occurred or apply oversimplifications to make things seem better or worse than it is. However, the heart of their narrative is generally accurate. If they receive a bad rating from the teacher, the manipulators can embellish the storyline by claiming that the poor grades were provided on purpose. The truth is because the trickster would not prep for the exam, which is why he received a poor score.

When it comes to manipulation, manipulators employ a variety of tools, including mimicry. The manipulator typically adopts an identity that is similar to but not identical to their own. They could offer a similar concept to someone else's and reward him with coming up with it first. This type of enhancement should be able to keep up with the speed of visual and auditory stimulation

The last tactic we'll look at is a diversion, a type of simulation used in deception when the trickster wants to have the victim's mind diverted from the facts to something else.

3.4. Detecting Deception

If you're searching for legal defenses against deceit, the initial step is to get an open mind that helps you to spot deception while it's being implemented. Ascertaining whether or not fraud is taking place can be complicated.

It is so because the trickster is a little clumsy in his strategy and leaves enough breadcrumbs to prove that he is still a master of grips and assertions contradiction. As daunting as it can be for a trickster to trick his target for a prolonged time, we do it regularly on those nearest to us. Deception is difficult to diagnose, and there are no firm markers that can be used to determine whether or not deception has occurred.

On the other hand, deception may significantly strain the manipulator's cognitive ability when they must work out how to remember all of the statements, they made to the victim to maintain the narrative believable and accurate. If one makes a mistake, the subject will claim that anything is inaccurate. The investigator is far more likely to spill facts to tip the subject by nonverbal or verbal signals due to the pressure of holding the story right. Studies have given us enough evidence to conclude that identifying a fraud attempt is normally a perceptual, fluid, and dynamic operation. These systems aren't always consistent, and they change based on the message being conveyed. Deception, according to the relational deceit theory, is an incremental and challenging experience of control among the trickster, whose main objective is to manipulate information into a narrative that ideally fits them but is not the reality, and the victim, who will then try figuring out whether the message becoming conveyed to them is accurate or indeed the con.

The perpetrator will help illuminate all of the verbal and non-verbal cues that will alert the victim of the deception during this specific stage.

The victim will be willing to say that the trickster is lying to them at some point during the operation.

Alert Vrij, one of the most respected experts on deceit, shares his perspective on deception identification. He believed there were no established non - verbal traits that could be linked purely to deceit. One of the main reasons that it is impossible to know whether someone is lying is this. While some nonverbal signals are correlated with deceit, these same cues may appear while other attitudes are involved.

This is why, unless a manipulator tells a blatant lie, determining whether or not they are using manipulation is impossible. Mark Fank is another author who has weighed in on the mysterious topic of detection. He concentrated on how deceit can be identified at the emotional stage of the witness. When someone is deceiving you, it normally involves intentional, calculated behavior on the victim's part, so responding to words and giving attention to the facial expressions that are happening is crucial when attempting to figure out whether they are deceiving you. Suppose a dishonest person, for example, poses a question that the victim does not feel safe addressing explicitly. In that case, you may say they are misleading from the way he emphasizes sentences often, has a low reasoning structure and spends less time thinking about that specific question. In general, there aren't many signals to remember when trying to find out when fraud happens. There are certain nonverbal signals that someone is using this manipulation technique. However, they may also be dealing with other problems such as shyness or nervousness.

Chapter 4: Manipulation and Techniques of Manipulation

In this chapter, we'll look at manipulation and what can be used to influence how "the subject" feels. Although the individual using deception is unlikely to be in jeopardy, it is designed to operate in a misleading and devious manner to alter the intended subject's actions, perspective, and opinion about a specific object or issue.

4.1. Definition of Manipulation

The main query that pops up is, "What is manipulation?" We will address manipulation in the context of psychological manipulation in this book, a social force that uses violent, misleading, or devious techniques to alter the attitudes or views of others or the victim. Most of the manipulator's tactics can be called misleading, cunning, violent, and oppressive because they are working to promote their objectives, especially at the costs of others. Although social power is not inherently bad, it can affect them when used to intimidate others or a party. Social control, such as that exerted by a physician trying to convince their patients to keep practicing healthier lifestyles, is often regarded as benign. It is valid to any social power that respects those concerned to make their own decisions and is not excessively authoritarian.

On the other hand, external influence can be negative and is usually frowned upon if anyone attempting to have their preferred way and manipulating others against their consent Persuasion and bullying are both used as forms of psychological or emotional manipulation. Bullying and brainwashing are two examples of elements that can be used in this type of mind control. The majority of people will perceive this as violent or misleading. People who want to manipulate others do so to control the actions of others around them. The manipulator will have a specific final objective in view and employ different means of violence to entrap those surrounding them into assisting the manipulator in achieving that goal. Emotional blackmail is sometimes used.

Mind management, brainwashing, or intimidation techniques are used by others who practice coercion to get people to perform assignments for them. The manipulator's target does not want to do the job, but they believe they have no other choice because of the threat or other technique. Since most deceptive individuals lack the necessary empathy and compassion towards others, they do not see their behavior.

Some manipulators are only obsessed with getting to their end target and are unconcerned with whoever has been inconvenienced or harmed along the route. Furthermore, deceptive people are always unable to enter a stable relationship for fear of being rejected by others. A manipulative personality is characterized by an inability to accept responsibility for one's behavior, difficulties, and life. Since they are incapable of taking responsibility for these matters, the manipulator may use deception techniques to get someone else to do so.

4.2. Techniques of Manipulation

In this section, we'll go into the most popular psychological conditioning tactics adopted by people who want to hurt you or take benefit of you. It's critical to comprehend these tactics and how they act to recognize them when they're being utilized towards you or anyone near to you, however, and that you can protect yourself.

A. Gaslight

One of the most dangerous social warfare tactics is gaslighting. It's when a manipulator attempts to persuade their victim to begin doubting their entire facts. It entails convincing others to dismiss their previous views and experiences, favoring accepting what else the manipulator wishes them to accept. The trickster will plant seeds of uncertainty in the person's mind, leading them to believe that they're just forgetting things or losing their minds. Gaslighting is described as the constant rejection of apparent evidence. There's still a lot of deception, lies, and outright deceit. When individuals are exposed to gaslighting for an extended period, they become psychotic and begin to believe that their convictions are unconstitutional. If you step into a room intending to talk about something specific but then notice yourself communicating with your mate about anything completely different, that's an indication that the individual is purposefully undermining your sincere attempts to connect. It may be an indication of gaslighting.

Gaslighting, in a nutshell, is the process of de-sensitizing you to your actual reality before the fact appears what the other party thinks it is.

B. Projection

Projection is a social ruse in which someone projects their feelings and faults into you. Projection is a type of protection that almost everybody employs to some degree. We also have an inherent propensity to transfer our negative thoughts and unfavorable feelings into those surrounding us, especially when we feel pressured. However, narcissists and those with other dark personality characteristics are more likely to do so frequently and at absurd levels.

Toxic people have a hard time admitting to themselves

whether the bad things that happen to them may be the product of their actions, and they still want someone to criticize for all. People like this go to great lengths to stop accepting accountability for their personal decisions. As a consequence, they can blame you for their negative tendencies and behaviors. If your employer is still late to work, for example, you could be shocked to see him blaming you for lateness regardless you are always on time.

C. Isolation

We ought to have social support networks to assist us in dealing with stressful times and prevent us from making poor choices. Friends and relatives recognize whether we switch our attitudes or probably hang out with bad folks, and they still have an eye on us.

Manipulators are aware of this, and most of the main things they'll do if they want to take hold of your life are detach you.

Isolation encourages bullying because it eliminates all redress you may have if anyone was violent. It reduces a victim's options for survival and heightens their feeling of powerlessness. It means that no one can come to the aid if things go wrong, and it gives the perpetrator or trickster more control over the victim by making the victim more reliant on the perpetrator.

Both types of manipulators often use the victim's isolation from the external world. When a group leader wants to subjugate new followers, he will lock them up so he'll have full leverage of the knowledge they get. In unhealthy relationships, workplace abuse, and a variety of other situations, the same thing happens.

D. Positive Reinforcement

Positive reinforcement is mostly thought of as a beneficial thing, and evil individuals can use it to exploit their victims. Positive affirmation is something that we all do in one way or another. Parents use it to get their children to act better, teachers to get their pupils enrolled in school, employers to inspire success, and couples to change one another's attitude in marriages. It's an important element of our social experiences, so it remains a threat when it harms the individual with which it's being used.

When a successful or attractive stimulus is delivered so that it seems to be a result of certain actions, this is known as positive reinforcement. A kid who eats his vegetables, for instance, receives a handful of ice cream at the end of the dinner, and it occurs to him that the two are inextricably related. A worker who performs well and becomes more profitable is rewarded with an incentive at the month-end. Their brain recognizes the connection between their hard graft and the additional money. Later, the person needs to do the same task; he or she will remember the good feeling or encouragement previously and assure a similar result.

E. Negative reinforcement

Negative reinforcement has become a type of social conditioning in which individuals feel compelled to behave in these ways to prevent emotional or physical harm or distress. Will have an incentive for handling the situation in the manner the manipulator wishes you to behave in positive reinforcement. The motivation for such a reward is just what changes your actions in the future. Negative affirmation, on the other hand, is a little more complex.

To get the idea of negative reinforcement, it's essential first to comprehend how it differs from punishment. Both are widely used deception methods. However, there is a distinction between them. Some people mistakenly believe they are identical, but they aren't really. If you don't respond in a particular manner, the manipulator applies something unpleasant to the punishment. If you behave the way the trickster wants you to behave, the manipulator takes away anything harmful. Reinforcement strengthens desirable answers, whereas punishment diminishes cooperative answers; the manipulator will prefer one option over the other depending on the kind of result they want in that situation.

F. Punishment

Punishment is a punitive move performed by the trickster to undermine the victim's voluntary reactions in psychological coercion. Punishment succeeds since it leaves the victim fearful of the repercussions of defying the manipulator's wishes. We've already discussed how punishment varies through negative reinforcement, but it's worth noting that the two will also intersect.

G. Nagging

Nagging, also recognized as hounding or browbeating, is a type of manipulation in which one person repeatedly encourages others to do anything despite the other person's refusal or agreement to do it later.

One author describes nagging as an encounter in which one person makes a repetitive demand. In contrast, the other person constantly refuses the request, and both parties become irritated as the clash of wills escalates.

Nagging, including its negative connotations, is an important aspect of interpersonal contact in many social situations. Parents nag their children and get them to do things they don't want to do. In reality, nagging is required when teaching children to develop positive behaviors. Well-intentioned people will nag you to perform stuff that benefits you; friends or spouses will pester you to do tasks that help you. In reality, even in happy marriages, some nagging is appropriate. Individuals with dark personality characteristics, on the other hand, will nag you to do stuff that helps them but harm you.

H. Yelling

Yelling acts as a manipulative tactic for one particular

reason: it leaves you feeling insecure or frightened, causing you to do whatever the manipulator wishes. Manipulators use shouting in two different ways to manipulate people. People scream to either control you or to portray the villain to win attention.

Anyone can be intimidated by yelling. When a malicious person shouts at you, he might be attempting to threaten you, knowing that you are much more inclined to do what they need if you are scared of them. Manipulative people turn to shout partially as they feel they can't make a compelling case to persuade you to do whatever they want right away. They realize that once you stick to the truth, you could win, but they scream to confuse you and cause you to drop the debate by default.

I. Silent treatment

Since it is a form of affection removal, the silent treatment acts as a deception tactic. "I'm stripping away the affection until you do what I need to," a person who brings others the silent treatment is saying. It's a means of punishment used to keep people under control, and it's a common form of mental violence. The silent treatment only occurs because both partners are emotionally dependent on one another (you don't mind if a stranger gives the silent treatment). The silent treatment could be utilized to help you feel helpless and worthless in some situations, as though you don't even exist.

To flourish as social creatures, we require the recognition and love of others.

Also, introverts require some form of involvement to the persons in society to feel complete. When anyone shows you the silent treatment, they deny you love, which may have social consequences and cause you to make sacrifices you aren't willing to make.

As a result, a trickster will demand you to be doing anything, and if you refuse, he or she will begin to ignore

you. They didn't respond to your calls or emails, and they didn't listen if you speak to them. Many of them can also disappear from your world or make an effort to stop even in the same place as you. The farther intensely engaged you are, the further likely it is that you will feel that holding your stance isn't worthwhile, and you will end up accepting what they need.

J. Intimidation

Intimidation may be subtle or overt, but manipulators use it in all cases to force you to bow to their every need out of fear.

Bullying is another term for overt coercion. Manipulators use open warnings to force you to do as they intend. They'll scare you into silence by instilling terror in you. It could be a danger of physical harm. They'll display their frustration and indignation to show you that they're violent. If you refuse to back down, they will turn to physical abuse.

They are commonly enraged individuals and have issues with authority.

The usage of hidden or ambiguous warnings to intimidate people is known as covert coercion. People who use subtle threats have aggressive impulses, but they manage to keep them in check since public signs of aggression are frowned upon in society. Such individuals are highly hazardous as they are adept at concealing their real identity from the entirety of society. These are the types of individuals who harass their wives at home but view themselves as charismatic to the outside world

Convert intimidators are usually very organized, or they are skilled at devising devious ways to threaten you if you don't do whatever they want.

K. Traumatic One trial learning

One-trial learning leads to individual interactions that we have that form our future behavior. This type of event is typically traumatic and strong enough to keep people from behaving in a certain manner for the remainder of their lives.

One-trial learning will happen without someone causing or forcing it on us in many ways. For instance, if you taste a new cuisine for the first time and have a severe case of food toxicity, you might be traumatized to the extent that you stop consuming the food in the future

Humans and animals alike benefit from one-trial learning because it is essential for life. Once we were only hunter-gatherers and hunters, one-trial learning would help us escape toxic foods and risky conditions.

One-trial learning is a deception tactic used by malicious individuals to get us to follow those lines. They do this by inducing the emotional memory so that our minds equate specific behavior with the trauma.

L. Manipulation of facts

Since it is founded on evidence that can be interpreted, truth manipulation is one of the most powerful psychological manipulation strategies. When anyone manipulates data, they are not explicitly talking crap; they utilize the truth to their advantage. It could include cherry-picking facts, eliding information, or excluding information from context.

Sometimes, the most incontrovertible evidence can be interpreted, and individuals with dark personality characteristics are adept at bringing up explanations that paint themselves in the greatest conceivable way that Machiavellians are particularly adept at manipulating facts make negative things appear to be healthy.

Making excuses is one way to distort reality in intimate relationships. People can justify all kinds of bad conduct by inventing scenarios that distort the meaning of their objectionable acts.

Blaming the perpetrator for his or her victimization is another way to distort evidence. Many known examples exist where abusers in marriages were trying to persuade the targets that they deserved to be abused because they did such activities. Most wife abusers justify themselves by arguing, "You forced me to do it." After the survivor has been removed from their support network, this coercion tactic also works better.

M. Creating an illusion

In addition to deceit, the manipulator will be skilled at building deceptions to help them achieve their end target more quickly. They will work to construct the image they desire and then persuade the victim that this vision is real, whether it is irrelevant to the manipulator. To accomplish this, the manipulator will amass the proof required to make the argument that serves their purpose. To begin the deception, the manipulator will implant ideas and facts into the subject's mind. When these strategies are in action, the manipulator will take a few days off and let the deception take place in the subject's mind at that moment. Afterward, the trickster has a good opportunity of persuading the target to follow the strategy.

N. Putting others down

If the manipulator wishes to enlist the help of their target in achieving the end objective, they have other choices. Once the trickster is ready to lay their subject down, this is a very effective tactic. When a manipulator uses rhetorical skills to bring their victim down, they run the threat of letting the victim feel as though they are being attacked personally. When a target feels threatened, they may become irritated and unable to help the manipulator in the manner that they want. Alternatively, the target will dislike the trickster and want to be as distant from them as possible, making the manipulator's ultimate objective very challenging to achieve. It is the reason why the trickster would not just go about putting their subject down. They must be more cautious about the procedure to figure a way to carry this out despite triggering warning signs or making the target feel victimized. Satire is one method for accomplishing this. Since comedy is amusing and lets people feel good, it can help break down walls that may otherwise arise. The manipulator is willing to make a joke out of their provocation. Regardless of the reality that the insult has been made into a joke, it would perform just as well as if it had not been converted into a joke, despite leaving noticeable scars on the target.

O. Leading questions

These questions are meant to guide the victim on a certain positive or negative path.

Leading questions in the workplace may include, "Do you have any problems with the project?" or "Did you like working on the project?" The former secretly encourage the victim to give a pessimistic response, while the latter encourages them to give a constructive response. You'll get a more reasonable answer if you ask, "How did you progress on in that task?"

Leading questions can also have a final appeal intended to persuade the target to cooperate with the speaker. 'This task is progressing well, isn't it?' for instance, it prompts the target to tell 'yes.' This is especially effective because, socially, we want to say yes to no. So, if we're faced with a choice, we'll normally go with the earlier.

4.3. Behavioral Traits Of The Manipulator

One of the most valuable coping strategies you need now is the ability to recognize whether someone is reaping the benefits of you or exploiting you. Everybody seems to have their desires and motivations, so it's important to know whether such intentions are sinister or will trigger damage unintentionally. Manipulators exhibit various behavioral and personality characteristics; several of them will be covered in this section. You'll be able to say whether or not an individual is a trickster, if or not their style of deception is intended to hurt you, and what sort of trickster they are using the knowledge you've learned here.

When you think someone is a manipulator, look into the following personality and behavioral characteristics.

A. Deception through lying

A "classic fib" is a lie committed on purpose. A deception of commission occurs if somebody states anything which they believe isn't true. Alternatively, a commission deception is anything false. It entails misleading others and telling them what they don't want to hear. It is highly deliberate, with the primary goal of gaining a personal benefit in a particular scenario.

The commission's lying isn't necessarily done maliciously, but those who feel more at ease saying overt lies are much more prone to be manipulators. Everybody deceives you. Even apparently naive small kids will say a commission lie to avoid getting into trouble; a boy with gum on his lip will deny rubbing it to avoid the repercussions of revealing the truth, not that he is evil.

Once you experience time with a trickster, you'll find that he regularly lies, particularly when the scenario doesn't call for it. Sadists will lie to inflict you harm, and narcissists will lie to make you think favorably of them. Commission lies can seem meaningless to you in some cases, but they still have a meaning for the trickster, even though you can't see it.

B. Lying by omission

Discriminatory detailing is another term for lying by omission. It entails saying the facts while omitting precise information. It could also mean failing to correct misunderstandings that one is knowledgeable of. Lies of omission are somewhat more subtle than lying of commission as they have a way out if the individual is caught lying. And in legal cases, you can get away with lying through omission, and you can often claim that the individual who posted the question wasn't clear enough about the information they needed you to include. The type of lying by omission that includes leaving out information is initial and very common. The greatest description of this kind of deception is when a salesperson touts a product's benefits while omitting to note its drawbacks. Manipulators may use omission lies to manipulate people's reactions in certain circumstances.

C. Denial

If you claim somebody is in denial, you're implying that they're having trouble recognizing the truth. When it comes to manipulators, indeed, denial brings a new sense. Tricksters employ denial to appear innocent while they are well aware that they may have committed a crime.

Tricksters employ denial to manipulate other people's perceptions of what they're doing and how they did it. Any manipulators are so skilled at utilizing denial that they can persuade others to begin second-guessing them. Denial is an important personality characteristic to look for when determining whether anyone will emotionally manipulate you. If your boyfriend flatly rejects everything you both consider to be real in the initial stages of your partnership, you can bet he'll be lying all the time to you in the coming years.

D. Avoidance

In a situation where direct responses are needed, evasion entails giving rambling or unnecessary input. When deceptive people are asked straightforward questions, they begin to chat about unrelated topics connected to the topic at hand.

Evasion is when someone tries to resist offering a direct answer to a question they've been asked. An individual who uses avoidance, on either hand, will evade the question or push the discussion differently. Avoiding a subject by bringing up a new one, particularly one that would likely elicit anger, is known as avoidance.

E. Rationalization

Making excuses is equivalent to rationalization. Manipulative individuals are masters at concocting stories to explain their treatment of others. When confronted with the most serious allegation, a trickster will react with a very well and persuasive justification for their behavior. When common folks rationalize or make reasons for their behavior, you have the impression that they are feeling ashamed and even regretful for whatever they have done, even if they are attempting to relieve their guilt. When tricksters rationalize their actions, they attempt to control how you view them, and they believe their actions are acceptable.

F. Playing victims

Manipulators never consider them as victims while they take on the part of the victim. For them, that's just a play, and the aim is to resist taking action while reaping the rewards of sympathy. For the reasons of evoking attention or managing impressions, they want to be viewed as vulnerable victims who are hurting, mentally damaged, or even physically hurt.

Manipulators attempt to persuade the targets that they'll be the ones failing in every way. If the victim cares for the manipulator's wellbeing, they will decide to help, even if it comes at a significant personal cost.

G. Generate fear

By feeding your worries, manipulators will even kill your personality.

They'll continue nurturing your worries until they figure out what they're afraid of so they can hold them towards you. The more fearful we are, the lower our self-esteem becomes.

People who are manipulative like it because their victims have poor self-esteem for a variety of reasons. You've always used the phrase "if you wouldn't fight for something, you'll break for it." It is what the manipulators are banking on. They know that even if you're not using a positive self-image, they will take advantage of how you see yourself. They'll step over and build a replica of you that they can use once you begin to doubt who you are.

H. Create Insecurity

Malicious people want to kill your self-esteem in addition to draining your motivation. Unfortunately, there are a plethora of options available to them. As hard as we want to build our self-esteem from the inside, the truth persists that as social creatures, we place a lot of value upon what people think about us, which is where deceptive people get their power.

Manipulators will erode your self-esteem by carefully crafting words that are intended to attack and belittle you. Their sentences are normally deliberately crafted to either offend or annoy you, causing you to waste a significant amount of time deciphering what they say.

4.4. Recognition Of The Toxic Relationship

Everyone wants to be in such a relationship where they feel safe and secure, and they know their partner is happy. A manipulator may be aware of this but will use it for their nefarious purposes. By instilling feelings of insecurity and resentment in their bond, a manipulator ensures that their spouse is helpless. In an intimate relationship, this tactic ' is often used. It appears as one partner repeatedly warns others that they will abandon them. It is done to instill fear and uncertainty in the relation. Promised breakups, implied breakups, and real breakups that never happen are all part of this silly game. Breakups that aren't explicitly stated are known as implied breakups. Instead, the trickster drops clues now and then to make the companions distrust themselves. They will do this by making comments that explicitly exempt their companion from plans for the future. Promised breakups occur when a dark manipulator convinces their mate that they can end things with them in the coming years instead. "Don't worry; I didn't have to bother with this again as I'll be leaving shortly," for example, indicate a potential split. Promise breakups come somewhere between suggested and real breakups. When a dark manipulator suggests splitting up with their mate, whether by divorcing, splitting, or breaking up, but does not carry through, it is referred to as the promised divorce.

In comparison to the suggested and planned breakups, the real separation is the most serious. It occurs when a trickster plans to abandon their victim but does not ultimately leave. They may try to flee by packing their clothing and possessions, but they change their minds when they see the sorrow on their victim's faces.

4.5. Prevention From Being Manipulated

To stop being a target of manipulators, you must strengthen your defenses such that you are ready to counteract whatever coercive tactics they can use. The easiest way to strengthen your defenses is to work on improving your personality and determination. That being said, you must be cautious over how you construct your protections, and you don't want to impose limitations that prevent you from enjoying a fulfilling life

You can't, for instance, behave out of desperation to avoid being manipulated. You can't isolate yourself from the rest of the world to escape situations where anyone might try to reap the benefits of you. Note that the world is filled with dark personality characteristics which may have sinister motives, but behaving out of fear will not keep you safe. It can, in effect, make you more like a goal. Start by assuming that you can face tricksters head-on while developing your defenses, and you'll never flee or retaliate. By necessity, if you behave out of fear, you will fail.

4.6. Selection Of Favorite Victim For Manipulators

Those with dark psychology tendencies are well aware that such attributes and personality traits make them more susceptible to coercion. Since they are simple targets, they prefer to pick out targets who have certain same personality characteristics. Let's look at the characteristics of manipulators' favorite victims.

A. Emotional Insecure

Manipulators like to prey on victims that are physically vulnerable or insecure. Regrettably, those characteristics are easier to see even in strangers for these people, making it very easy for skilled manipulators to track them down.

B. Sensitive People

Extremely sensitive people perceive information profoundly and are better mindful of social processes' subtle nuances. They have several good characteristics since they are thoughtful of others and monitor their steps to prevent harming others, either direct or indirect. Those persons are quickly offended by news stories of tragic events or even representations of gratuitous gore in the film, and they hate any kind of abuse or brutality.

C. Empathic People

Assertive people are comparable to extremely emotional people, and they're more emotional to other people's feelings and the energy in the environment. They have a proclivity for internalizing other people's pain to the point where it becomes their own. In reality, for a few of them, distinguishing someone else's pain other than their own can be challenging. Emphatic people are the strongest friends, and they understand what you're going through. They are, however, especially easy to exploit as a result of this, which is why evil people like to attack them.

D. Fear of Loneliness

Many people are scared of being isolated, but only a limited population has this anxiety. This type of anxiety will paralyze those who feel it, leaving them vulnerable to abuse by unscrupulous individuals.

E. Personality Dependent Disorder

Those having dependent personality disorders are common targets for tricksters since they are easy to manipulate and conquer. Because these people voluntarily hand over control of their affairs to others, tricksters face no opposition as they come calling. Manipulators begin by instilling a false sense of security in them, but if they've gained their confidence, they shift gears and begin enforcing their control on them.

Are you enjoying this book? If so, I'd be really happy if you could leave a short review on Amazon, it means a lot to me! Thanks!

Click here if you want to know the TEN STRATEGIC AND POWERFUL SALES PERSUASION TECHNIQUES for Free →
http://bit.ly/10strategic

Chapter 5: Covert Emotional Manipulation

Recognizing subtle mental coercion is the initial step toward truly comprehending dark psychology as a whole. It is how all of the dark psychology approaches we'll discuss in this book involve subtle mental coercion in multiple ways. Reading more on this specific topic would enable you to interpret better what it entails and recognize its different variations throughout the globe. As a result, this is a critical phase in comprehending the larger field in dark psychology.

5.1. Definition of Covert Emotional Manipulation

It is described as an individual's effort to subtly but undetectably affect the feelings and thoughts of some other person. Tearing down each one of the three factors can help with the very foundation of this concept. The term "covert" specifically refers to how these tricksters can conceal their actual self and motives from their intended victim. However, not all emotional coercion should be classified as clandestine. In many other cases, the targets of this form of emotional coercion are unaware that they've been manipulated from the background. Neither are they sure of the manipulator's intentions for doing so.

The emotional component of this concept corresponds to the manipulator's singular emphasis. Deception of people's strengths, beliefs, and attitudes are common examples of other forms of manipulation. This method of deception focuses on influencing a person's state of mind and also their true experience. The bulk of manipulators focus on this region the most. It also leads to them thoroughly comprehending a person's feelings, which are the portal to all other dimensions of their character. As a result, the trickster has complete access to the target since the start.

Deception is the final step of this very complex game of covert manipulation. Manipulation is commonly confused, and it is often mistaken for power. It may not be even farther from reality, as coercion is often defined as a hidden mechanism of unfair power that occurs beyond the self-awareness of the person that has been subjected to control. They are often guided by distinct motives for both coercion and effect. A person who sees themselves as an endorser will frequently attempt to support a person in any way, but only in particular. A trickster is the exact opposite, as their goal is to subtly control their targets because of their benefit, usually without regard for the target. As a result, the motive is a crucial factor to consider when determining if a particular action is deceptive.

5.2. Techniques Of Covert Emotional Manipulation

Let's discuss the tactics of covert emotional manipulation.

A. Emotional intimidation

A manipulator can purposefully trigger you to provide an emotional breakdown and accuse you of being insane or beyond reach. The goal is to create a complicated and dramatic scene that will divert your attention away from a problem you brought up with the trickster. Rather, it's your evident cognitive dysfunction that's the problem. The trickster can also achieve more strength and leverage by using this strategy. Covert intimidation works on the same basis as blatant intimidation: it preys on a person's emotions. Fear is preyed upon by covert coercion, while sympathy is preyed upon by guilt-tripping. Covert-aggressive personalities are a term used by clinicians to describe those who employ these tactics. "Wolves in sheep's clothes," as they call themselves. They put on a good front to the outside world, but they are ruthless individuals on the inside.

Intimidating targets in a non-obtrusive manner is referred to as covert bullying. People related to you will do it whether they share your doubts or wishes.

Your employer can use subterfuge to persuade you to do their lobbying at work.

If they know you're pursuing a raise, he may demand you to do him favors and then say that your advancement is contingent on that favor. He does not mention it out loud, but it will all be in the background.

B. Triangulation

A manipulator's repertoire includes the deceitful and powerful technique of triangulation. A triangle is formed between you, him, and a third party beyond the relation by the trickster. It's meant to make you feel insecure in your friendship, making you want to appease the trickster to maintain him or her on. In any form, the trickster will put a male or female into the relation (intentionally or unintentionally). They could casually — and often — discuss an old acquaintance, a colleague, or anyone they see on their daily coffee run. Alternatively, they could be openly flirting with others in front of you. Their attraction to the other individual makes them feel insecure. It's made much worse if they draw subtle unfavorable associations among you and outside individuals, which they're prone to do.

If you approach them, they will dismiss all involvement in some other individual and claim that insecurity or poor self-esteem is the main issue. Where did you first read that?

It's not unusual for the trickster to be recruiting the other individual as their next goal while both are devaluing and manipulating you. For instance, the trickster can flirt with another female next to you to strengthen their relationship with her by forcing you to act envious and jealous, which can then be used to justify ending your partnership. You should recognize where you are with your mate in a stable relationship. A trickster maintains a sense of unpredictability.

C. The blame games

The manipulator uses this technique to blame the survivor for the troubles in the relation. This strategy effectively places you on the defensive (making you seem guilty) or convincing you that you are the one that is to blame. The manipulator will argue that they are the someone who is at fault as the relationship deteriorates and eventually ends. They can also persuade common friends and family members that you are at fault, causing them to switch towards you. You notice yourself with little to no help only when you need it the most. Expert manipulators often act as if they are, or have been, the target.

D. The bait and switch

Change the subject (also known as "bait and switch"). Pretend you're going to learn about the subject that makes you nervous before transitioning to something else. It functions well enough at work and much better at home. Your wife is worried about your drinking habits. "At least I'm not spending money buying as you are doing all the moment!" you respond. Oh yes! You don't have to worry because of your waste anymore; now, you should talk about hers when she isn't treating you well.

E. The law of state transference

Emotions are infectious, according to the rule of state transference. Consider a cute dog entering the room. His personality and vibe are sure to be infectious, in contrast to his good looks. Although a sufficient powerful emotion will often overpower social value, the individual with the higher level of social value AND the highest sentiment will dominate the transference. Since it is due to the artist's getting control over groups of individuals, state transference is a significant topic in Real Social Dynamic's seminars. It also implies that they will have the ability to influence how a female feels. The seduction is carried out through this impact canvas, which ends in the woman having intense, typically optimistic emotions toward the seducer.

F. Leading Questions

Asking leading questions is another technique that a skilled dark manipulator employ. Since they inquire about the target questions to elicit a certain range of answers, that could reasonably be interpreted as one of the most powerful linguistic tactics. A dark manipulator may, for instance, question their target, "How poor do you believe these folks are?" This problem implies that the people involved are unquestionably evil to some degree. Dark manipulators ask such leading questions so deftly that they know the target is agitated up to the point that they abandon the vessel and then return to the asking line until the victim seems to be calm. Dark manipulators often use their true motives to disguise their dark coercion. To avoid being quickly persuaded by dark manipulation, the manipulator conceals his real intent from the start, or they will lose. Based on the victim and circumstances, professional manipulators may hide their true motives in various ways. Individuals who interpret have a talent for dark manipulators. If you understand personality types in people, using reverse psychology to achieve whatever you want becomes easy.

G. Insinuation

Insinuation functions like this: a clue is thrown in the middle of a mundane comment or experience. It's regarding an emotional issue—possibly unfulfilled enjoyment, a lack of enthusiasm in one's existence. The clue is a sly jab at the target's insecurities that emerges throughout the background of the target's mind; the source is easily overlooked. It is too elusive to be remembered at the moment, so as it takes hold and spreads, it appears to have developed spontaneously from the target's consciousness as if it had already been there. Since the universe is often too boring, insinuation works. We yearn for something new and mysterious because of the little magic it has. We ask what the others are up to when they deviate from the norm and don't mention what they intend. We consider what they desire, and in this sense, we enter another world, outside of the tedious predictability enforced by our daily routines.

Remember, the insinuation is only effective when you're trying to entice somebody who isn't even interested in you.

Chapter 6: Persuasion and Its Methods

Another type of mind manipulation that will be addressed is persuasion. Although there isn't as much public attention given to this type of mind management as brainwashing or hypnosis, that might be just as successful if done properly. The problem with this type of persuasion is that it could be impossible for any particular channel to get it across the target and cause a change as there are multiple kinds of persuasion in everyday life. Although persuasion, like most ways of mind management, works to alter the subject's thoughts and opinions, it appears that someone is attempting to convince you over something, making it easy to resist the persuasion which is flowing at the subject. For instance, there is a kind of convincing going on in advertisements on tv, when a debate is heading on, and if a conversation is happening. Persuasion is sometimes used to one's benefit without the individual being aware of it. This chapter would go further into persuasion and be used successfully as a means of mind control.

6.1. Definition of persuasion

Persuasion is a dark psychology phenomenon that has a lot in common with manipulation. This is because they are both used to manipulate a victim's intentions, behavior, emotions, and values. There are various explanations why we use persuasion in our daily lives, but the most important is to bring people from opposing viewpoints together. Persuasion is a dynamic force that has a significant impact on the target and culture. It can be seen in everyday life. There have been some key distinctions among persuasion, and other ways of mind control explored in this book. To change the victim's mind and identity, brainwashing and hypnosis require the victim to be isolated. Manipulation may also be used on a single individual to achieve the desired result. Although persuasion can be used to convince a single person to reconsider their viewpoint, it is often feasible to use persuasion to a broader extent to persuade an entire population or even civilization to change their minds. It will make it much more powerful and possibly harmful since it can shift the opinions of a significant number of individuals at once instead of only a single person. Most people genuinely assume that they are resilient to the influence of persuasion. They believe that they might be ready to recognize every sales pitch tossed their way, regardless of whether the agent is marketing a product or a new concept, and then grasp the case and reach a decision with their reasoning.

6.2. Methods of persuasion

Now we have a good grip on what persuasion is, Now let us plunge headlong into the different persuasive methods that are open to everybody. These persuasion methods are often categorized under different terms and alluded to as persuasion tools and strategies. It's crucial to understand that there's no one-size-fits-all approach to persuading someone to behave and think in a particular way. The manipulator can communicate their target into presenting a certain kind of proof that is normally directed toward changing the subject's viewpoint, or they could be inclined to use coercion or force against the target. It places the target in a situation where they can either help the trickster or employ a different strategy. In the following pages of this series, examples of these strategies will be explored.

Tricksters usually bide their time wooing their targets and ensuring that they appreciate them to the extent where they gain the victim's confidence and trust. After this stable trust foundation has been built, the persuader begins to manipulate their targets.

A. Ethos

Ethos is an Ancient Greece word that means "character." Morality and credibility are the foundations of ethos appeals. It may involve obtaining key people's recommendations, establishing your professional reputation, and quoting expert evidence in a statement. To gain credibility, you must show everyone as a person of good morals, reliable, and knowledgeable about the subject of your conversation. The power to convince is linked to a person's or a report's honesty and authenticity and the audience's expectations of the speaker's trustworthiness. It refers to the speaker's ability to persuade the listener that they are competent to address (talk) the matter at hand. That can be achieved in a variety of ways: by becoming a prominent personality in the area in a discussion such as a college professor or an employee in a corporation whose profession would be same of the topic; by having a particular involvement in the subject like the person being connected to the subject at hand.

B. Pathos

Pathos is a convincing method that appeals to a listener's sense of self-identity, consciousness, and feelings. An audience responds to pathos verbally and by identifying with the author's viewpoint and understanding what the writer thinks. It can depend on the expectations and hopes of the audience. The persuader may create a state of openness to the proposals in them. They may try to elicit sympathy for someone or disdain for any wrongdoing from the audience. Fear, sympathy, pride, rage, and remorse are a few forms of emotions that occur in public speech.

Emotional arguments can also be challenging for some people as they require refined communication techniques, including using language effectively and emotionally. It's not easy to elicit passion from an audience by using auditory range rhythm and repetition.

C. Logos

Any effort to speak to the mind, i.e., persuading by logic, is referred to as logos. Logos refers to the language itself in the sense that it confirms or appears to prove something. It's usually used to explain statistics and figures that back up the speaker's assertions. Persuasion by words, not factual evidence, is what logos is all about. It's a demonstration that persuades the audience that the decision reached is the correct one for the situation. By using eye-catching 'logos,' the speaker demonstrates to the audiences that they are professional about the subject. The most critical facets of reputation appeals are the respective speaker's 'authoritativeness' and 'truthfulness' (Bradley, 1991). They contribute to the speaker's credibility, reputation, and ability to be trusted". 'Causal reasoning' is the interpretation through a particular to another, with the speaker attempting to demonstrate that something happens or may happen due to some other reason. Throughout this scenario, two forms of logic are used: result – to – trigger reasoning (once the speaker is reacting to past events) and cause – to – effect reasoning (once the speaker is relating to potential events) (when they are speeching about future ones)

'Statistics' backs up a point of various types of logos. The key is to the distinction between statistics and reality, as well as how to apply them. Some positions are backed by the expression "studies prove," even though the percentages used to justify a specific cause or argument are always not representative of the study's ultimate point.

The use of percentages to demonstrate how valuable one's commodity is known as statistics-based persuasion.

6.3. Techniques of Persuasion

If the individual wishes to be effective in persuading the target to do something, they may need to develop certain tactics to assist them. Every day, the target would be subjected to various means of persuasion. Food manufacturers will try to persuade the subject to buy new goods, while studios will promote their newest blockbusters. Since convincing can be sought almost everywhere, it would be difficult for the manipulator to persuade others of their perspective on the matter. Persuasion methods have been noticed and practiced for thousands of years, dating back to antiquity. Since control is so beneficial to a wide range of individuals, this has been achieved. Since the early twentieth century, there has been a systematic analysis of these methods.

Since the end aim of persuasion is to persuade the target to internalize the convincing argument and then accept it as a new mindset, determining which persuasion methods are the most effective has a lot of importance. The different negotiation methods that will be explored in this section are those that offer the greatest benefit to the agent.

A. The door in the face

Persuasion strategies differ, but there are a few that are pretty obvious. Others will go unnoticed, and these are the forms of convincing that are much riskier. So, how could individuals get other persons to do what they desire? Some would use the "foot in the door" strategy. Simply put, you can ask for a small favor before requesting a large one. It's easier to convince someone to answer yes, a second time after you've gotten them to answer yes, the first time. The smaller favor would complement the greater favor. Requesting someone to lose change when you lost it in your car because it's time for lunch is a classic example of this, followed by asking the victim to share the lunch because you didn't have it yourself.

B. Foot in the door

On the other hand, the door-to-face procedures are the polar opposite of the foot in the door theory. Instead of asking for something little, then something larger, you demand something large, then something small. This strategy is extremely effective. You can ask your closest friend for $10,000, and they will almost certainly say no. If they've done that, you can ask for a twenty, and they'll be far more likely to comply. This method of persuasion is risky, but it's easy to spot if you practice being aware of what others are doing and thinking. You should pay close attention to what they are doing or asking.

C. Yes- set trick

A persuasion procedure called a "yes package" entails the target responding "yes" to the therapist's advice. It's a 'chained' or arranged recognition response to help the victim effect improvement in the consulting room, some manipulator, for instance, using sophisticated means of contact. Suggestions may be 'chained' as an example of this type of contact. The trickster might say, for instance, "After you undergo (this), you will start to feel (that)." For a more precise illustration, consider this: 'As you continue to breathe more steadily, you will feel your body relaxing.'

When using manipulation, these chaining ideas are important. 'As the deception develops emphasis and traction, the main aim is to increase the target's responsiveness to the suggestions.' The 'Yes Package' is one of the most widely employed response sets, as well as the easiest way to set things up is for the manipulator to give the victim a series of truisms, each of which requires the target to respond with a nonverbal 'Yes.' The theory is that the victim automatically corresponds to each point when you make it. It is also beneficial to switch from specific observations to broader generalizations.

D. Linguistic presupposition

A presupposition is an assumption that exists before a statement is uttered. A presupposition sentence requires accepting a particular belief before the rest of the sentence can be interpreted or accepted as fact. Another term to consider is "assumption." A presupposition may be founded on a widely held assumption. Alternatively, the presupposition could not be valid at all (and that's where presuppositions may be hazardous). Presuppositions with no base in evidence can be seen all over the place in grammar. However, because of the "still" manner in which they are delivered, they are often overlooked by the audience and thereby assumed to be real. In reality, by confusing them with other evidence in your statement, you can persuade someone to accept a presupposition that they would otherwise doubt.

E. Reverse psychology

Reverse psychology has become a form of deception that is more refined. It is technically characterized as a persuasion strategy that involves asserting an opinion or action instead of needed, assuming that this tactic will persuade the coercion target to do what is ultimately desired. The main distinction between reverse psychology and deception is that the targeted individual is provided the illusion of preference. They are led to think that they will be making a conscious decision to do just what is their wish when they have indeed been persuaded to do just what the trickster desires. It's awesome when you consider the thought that goes into getting this off when you're in the victim's shoes.

Reverse psychology seems to be a parenting tool that parents often use to guide their kids. It's particularly effective with children who've been considered "aggressive" to authority. It seems to be harmless throughout the surface, with no apparent consequences for the infant or their mental health, but it has been documented to turn sour.

F. Blackmail

A manipulator's favorite tactic would be to use blackmail. Blackmail is described as an act in which the manipulator makes unjustified threats to obtain or inflict damage to the victim only if the manipulator's goal is achieved. It may also be described as a form of intimidation that includes threats of criminal action, risks of stealing the victim's property or assets, or threats of harming the subject physically. It is a tactic that the manipulator would be able to use to achieve what they desire. They'll spend some time learning personal information about their target, which they might then use as a means of blackmail. They can threaten to reveal a humiliating secret or jeopardize their likelihood of starting a better job or promotion by blackmailing their target. Alternatively, the manipulator may use a more aggressive approach, threatening to physically hurt their target or the subject's relatives if they refuse to cooperate with the trickster.

G. Love bombing

People's family bond is very powerful when it comes to Love Bombing. It is the band into which you were born and have essentially spent your entire life. They understand you more than anybody else, and those who haven't had the opportunity to get into this sort of relationship might seem lonely and unwelcome. By using emotional attachment, feeling, sharing, and physical contact, the agent can build a sense of belonging through love bombing. It creates a familial relationship between the agent and the subject, making it much easier to switch in the previous life for the current one.

H. Positive reinforcement

Positive reinforcement tactics include public recognition facial expressions (such as a forced smile), attention, gift items, permission, funds, inordinate apologizing, materialistic sympathy (including fake tears), grandiosity, and appreciation. This type of motivation aims to justify others to continue to have been your mate. Giving someone a gift or any money will make them more likely to assist you once the time finally comes. If you can make the target, feel bad for you, you'll get the sympathy you need to get them to support you afterward.

6.4. Empathy and Persuasion

To be specific, empathy is described as the capacity to comprehend what others are feeling, doing, and going through. You must first learn where somebody is to convince them. If you don't know where they've been heading, you can't guide them to a new destination. Since empathy works both ways, many people don't give themselves up to it. You may know someone else's point of view is true until you grasp it. You might discover that your simplistic stories regarding them aren't accurate. You might not be able to change their viewpoint, but yours will undoubtedly change. For instance, we suggest, "You can accompany me because of our mutual identity," and if you aren't of the same nation, my point would be ignored.

On the other hand, the point could be very convincing if your national heritage is very significant to your personality. Many of the points we used to make and see others make are based on the assumption that the other individual is the same as you, that they share your specific thoughts, emotions, and memories, and that they would respond to new knowledge in the same manner you do, rather than acknowledging their specific viewpoint and starting point. All those other persuasion tactics will succeed if you have empathy. However, once you understand where your audience is, you won't move and direct them. As a result, begin with empathy. Begin by really attempting to comprehend other 's thoughts, emotions, and memories. When you're not ready now, try practicing patience for your emotional neediness.

6.5. How To Influence & Persuade?

Being competent to convince and manipulate people to have what you intend is a crucial ability not just in business but also in life! Any contact between people is a means of communication. Nothing will be accomplished in the corporate sector until employers, staff, clients, vendors, and consumers effectively communicate with, influence, and persuade. When you look at the world's most influential entrepreneurs, you'll see that they've done such a good job of influence and convincing. That's the distinction between becoming a competent communicator and being an expert communicator: advanced communicators know how to manipulate and convince others and communicate through them. It necessitates a great deal of preparation, dexterity, and a skill range that is well above the normal people. Despite the importance of such skills and knowledge, many people feel that they have hit a peak of their ability to persuade and manipulate others and hit a roadblock in their development. They may find it difficult to communicate their opinions and beliefs accurately. They are often unable to comprehend what other person thinks or experiencing, and why they have been avoiding efforts to convince or manipulate them.

Most people may use abrasive or offensive tactics to impress and manipulate others. They will reach a consensus on occasion, but there may be fundamental, possibly passive, the discord that impacts the team. Actual persuasion and power entail persuading someone of the value of your proposals without having to threaten or insult them. Rather, you learn to identify what a certain person needs to listen and feel, seeing in response to being convinced. Then you'll be capable of delivering the missed information or contact in a manner that the other party will understand.

6.7. Persuasion Techniques In Business

You're a hardworking developer who is still looking for new customers and ways to increase revenue. You could have attempted many times to adjust the price packages, add more offerings, or even taking on more clients to increase your revenue. But the art of convincing, which is a science, was certainly never learned in Business School. And I'm sure nobody ever informed you how effective persuasive methods would be in persuading more customers to purchase to you and more employers to accept the plan or contract if they're applied correctly.

So, let's take a look at those primary convincing methods you might use right now.

- **The art of reciprocity**

If someone does anything for you or sends you something, it's normal for you to feel obligated to repay the favor. It's the same in industry, and you should start using it.

- **Start small but be consistent**

This technique is based on the fact that individuals have a stable pattern of actions. As a result, after the client has reached a decision, they are more likely to act in ways compliant with that decision.

- **Social proof**

If you've ever purchased a product, you did not know before landing on their sales website, consider what prompted you to do so.

Most people would do or buy what someone else is doing or buying, particularly when they have no previous experience to base their decision on. That's why testimonials, whether written, film, or feedback, are among the most effective and widely used sales tactics.

- **Celebrity Status**

Though becoming a celebrity isn't required to command a lot of publicity, gain more confidence, or have more authority, it certainly helps! As a result, you will gain this position by establishing yourself as the go-to individual in your business.

- **Less is more**

Often customers desire something they can't get and

making the goods and services more limited or elusive would do just that.

- **Putting your skills to the test**

You will see a change and progress throughout your client relations if you look at any of these approaches and adapt them to your present way of working.

You'll draw potential customers and references as a consequence of practicing the art of convincing existing clients that you can persuade them to continue working with you.

6.8. Persuasion by mass media and advertisement

People currently live in a consumerist society. People are overwhelmed by various brands every day and are bombarded by ads from television, the web, newspapers, banners, and other sources. People dream about the amazing new toy they purchased last weekend, and what appears to be a harmless play turned out to be just another advertisement for a well-known brand's new update.

Of course, we all buy first and foremost to meet our needs. Since there can be such a wide range of goods available nowadays, advertisers have had to be creative to persuade consumers to buy their product in the last few decades. Advanced marketing experts are very well acquainted with many of the previously mentioned latent drivers and psychological elements that influence purchasing decisions. We may not realize it, but still, almost every commercial today contains a subversive or supraliminal message or is made using attention-getting stimuli. This marketing power begins in childhood and accompanies each person during their everyday life. In this segment, we'll go over the most common persuasion strategies used in marketing and advertising, as well as details of how companies are using them in their promotions.

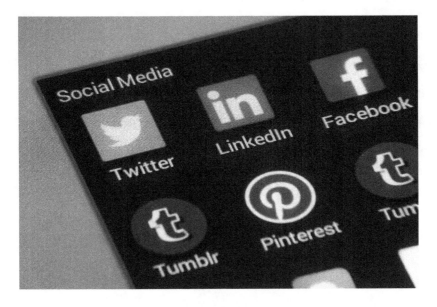

- **Persuasion by Images**

The strength of our sighs and sensory perception regions of the brain is immense. Consider this for a moment: have you ever spoken about anyone without picturing how they appear? Due to which, this the media prefers storytelling and graphic manipulation as a means of communication. Companies also use split-second photographs of a product or an entity in advertisements that seem harmless at first glance. It is often referred to as subliminal coercion. These split-second videos, which are normally presumed by the most part, typically end up gaining control of the customer, persuading them to buy the specific service.

- **Persuasion by Sound**

The use of sound in the convincing of innocent captives is yet another technique used by the media. Some people tend to underestimate the influence of sound. But remember, how often have do you listen to a jingle somewhere to have it play over and over in your head?

Songs normally affect all of us as though we are unaware of it, considering that we are known that people are listening to them. It is something that the media often exploits in their efforts to persuade the public. A variety of words will also be skillfully disguised and replicated in a commercial number that will most probably persuade you to choose a certain brand over the other. McDonald's is an excellent demonstration of this. The song "I'm lov'in it" is frequently played to encourage the victims to buy their food regularly.

6.9. Persuasion in intimate relations

There is indeed a variety of interpersonal coercion in intimate relationships, though it isn't necessarily intentional. It's natural for females to want to change men's behavior to make them more "house trained." There are a few cases of coercion in which the person's motive is apparent and driven by a need to manipulate or overpower the opponent.

In intimate relationships, positive thinking may be the most often employed hidden conditioning tactic. Your husband will persuade you to do what he wishes by praising you, rewarding you, paying close attention to you, sending you presents, and behaving affectionately. Even the items that seem pleasant in a relationship may be seen as persuasion mechanisms and props. Your partner, for example, could use extreme sex as a tactic to promote a particular type of behavior in you. Men may also use charisma, affection, and gifts to reinforce those habits in the girls they date.

To maintain control of their mates, most professional persuaders do whatever psychologists label "intermittent positive reinforcement." The attacker showers the survivor

with a constant positive affirmation for some time before returning to the usual amount of attention and gratitude. They will return to the strong positive reinforcement after a specific period. Until the victim becomes accustomed to the special consideration, it is removed. When they become accustomed to a regular response, the preferential privileges are reinstated, much of which seems to be unreasonable. Still, the survivor will reach a point where she is "addicted" to the special privileges. Still, they no clue how to get it, so they begin doing whatever the persuader requests to hope that one of their actions will result in the return of the strong positive reinforcement. Negative reinforcement strategies are often used to influence people in relationships subtly. Spouses, for instance, may withdraw intimacy to force the other partner to change their behavior in a certain way.

Click here if you want to know the TEN STRATEGIC AND POWERFUL SALES PERSUASION TECHNIQUES for Free →

http://bit.ly/10strategic

Chapter 7: Hypnosis, Its Types, and Uses

Although many people have heard about brainwashing, hypnosis is another vital method of mind control to remember. The majority of users related to hypnosis have learned about this from live performances where actors perform absurd acts.

Although it is a kind of hypnosis, it is far more than that. This chapter would focus mostly on hypnosis as just a method of mind management.

7.1. Definition of Hypnosis

To begin, let's look at the concept of hypnosis. According to scholars, hypnosis is a phase of consciousness marked by the subject's enhanced capacity to react to feedback while involving focused concentration and decreased peripheral perception. It ensures that the client may reach a new frame of mind to be far more receptive to the hypnotist's advice. It is generally acknowledged that there have been two principal classes that explain what occurs throughout hypnosis. The altered state hypothesis is the first of these. According to this theory, hypnosis is similar to a coma or distorted mental state in which the person would find that their consciousness is unique from what else they can feel in their normal waking state. The non-state hypotheses are the other kind of theory. Many who believe in this hypothesis believe that hypnotized people should not experience distinct levels of consciousness. Instead, the client collaborates with the hypnotherapist to engage in the form of creative role play.

The client has increased focus and attention while under hypnosis and a new capacity to focus on a particular memory or feeling constantly. Therefore, the participant can prevent some other factors that may be disruptive during this phase. Subjects that have been hypnotized are believed to have a greater capacity to respond to recommendations, particularly when the suggestions originate from the hypnotherapist. The method of inducing hypnosis in an individual is classified as a hypnotic induction, and it entails a sequence of recommendations and guidelines that serve as a warm-up.

Experts have several different ideas about what hypnosis is and how to define it. The vast range of these meanings stems from the idea that there are so many common situations that can accompany hypnosis, and no two will have the same reaction while under it.

7.2. Types of Hypnosis

The subject would be able to see a variety of various forms of hypnosis. Most of them will operate in a somewhat different manner, and others will assist with many topics. Others may be better suited to assist the subject in relaxing, and some may be better suited to assist in losing weight or pain control. This segment would go through the various forms of hypnosis that are accessible in greater depth.

- **Traditional Hypnosis**

Traditional hypnosis is by far the very common form of hypnosis that is used. The agent is merely giving recommendations to the victim's unconscious minds throughout that phase. This form of hypnosis would be more effective on a subject that is noted for believing what they have been told and not asking many questions. When you go to a trained hypnotist or buy a tape to perform self-hypnosis, you would be engaging in conventional hypnosis. The popularity of this form of hypnosis stems from the fact that it requires no skill or instruction to master. The hypnotist would only need to make a brief script to direct the subject's actions. This approach works well for people who embrace what is happening out there, but it fails to work on people who think objectively and analytically.

- **Ericksonian Hypnosis**

Ericksonian Hypnosis is the next form of hypnosis to be explored. This one would involve metaphors and short stories, but it will be a bit further in. It is used to communicate the required ideas and advice to an unconscious mind. About the fact that this approach necessitates a bit more experience and preparation, it is a very useful and efficient method to employ. It is effective as it can remove any resistance or obstruction that the subject might have with the recommendations.

- **Embedded Technique**

The embedded technique is another form of hypnosis. The hypnotherapist will tell the topic a fascinating tale during this time. This narrative is intended to help the subject's conscious mind be distracted and engaged. It will also provide subtle ideas concealed within the plot but will be embraced by the subject's unconscious mind. The hypnotist can use process guidance to guide the subject's unconscious mind to the recollection required through this narrative. This recollection is normally of a relevant learning event from the past. Therefore, the hypnotist would be capable of using that knowledge to assist them with making progress in their current situation.

- **Nero-Linguistic Programming**

The hypnotist would be encouraged to employ the same thinking processes that are causing the difficulty in the victim by using NLP. As opposed to going through the recommendation process, this will save a lot of time.

- **Video Hypnosis**

Although other types of hypnosis have proven to be effective in helping people conquer challenges and change their minds to live a fulfilling lifestyle, different hypnosis techniques are constantly being created.

Video hypnosis is one of the more recent types of hypnotherapy to emerge. This form is made available by commercial channels so that consumers can buy it and use it wherever they want. The approaches used in video hypnosis are also based on the Neuro-Linguistic Programming technology previously explored. It suggests that instead of using hypnotic suggestions as conventional approaches, the video hypnosis approach would succeed by using the subject's internal thought patterns.

- **Subliminal Hypnosis**

Subliminal hypnosis is the final method of hypnosis that will be explored in this chapter. The subliminal hypnosis signals are frequently recorded and played back to the subject. The tape will consist of two tracks, each of which will address a particular aspect of the mind. A cover sound can be heard from the subject's thinking mind on one of the tracks. Nature sounds or songs are sometimes used as the cover sound since they are great to listen to by the brain. The other track will include clear feedback that the subject will hear from their unconscious mind. These ideas, which can be found on the second track, will be repeated during the course.

7.3. Uses Of Hypnosis

Hypnosis, both as a profession and as a concept, has a long history. As a result, numerous applications that help bring the hypnosis technique to effective use have started to arise. In reality, hypnosis has a wide range of applications, including entertainment, self-improvement, military applications, and medical applications. Rehabilitation, physical therapy, education, recreation, and forensics are some of the other fields that have increasingly started to use hypnosis. Even performers have started to use hypnosis to achieve those artistic goals.

Some of the most common applications of hypnosis would be in the area of self-improvement; often, people use it to help themselves shed pounds, relieve stress, and stop smoking. The parts that follow will go into some of the various areas that hypnosis has already been expanding and how the hypnosis method works in those areas.

- **Hypnotherapy**

Hypnotherapy is a type of meditation that involves the use of hypnosis. It is employed to support patients or subjects in overcoming troublesome problems, particularly where other forms of self-control have failed. Authorized psychiatrists and doctors may use hypnotherapy to treat posttraumatic stress disorder, compulsive gambling, sleep disturbances, eating disorders, anxiety, and depression in willing patients.

- **Military Applications**

People have long asked why hypnotherapy is being used by military and state authorities to transform the way civilians think about things, in addition to helping people with different health conditions and addictions. So far, there has been no evidence that the US military can or has been using hypnosis to achieve its objectives. In reality, according to a newly declassified paper accessed via the Freedom of Information Request archive, the technique of hypnosis has been tested to be used for military purposes. Despite the analysis, the report found no proof that hypnosis could be effective in military situations. Furthermore, there was no proof that hypnosis existed as a separate condition from subject anticipation, high optimism, and ordinary suggestion.

- **Self-hypnosis**

When a licensed hypnotherapist or other expert is unavailable, you may want to use the self-hypnosis method. When individuals are inclined to hypnotize themselves, mostly with the use of autosuggestion, this process happens. The main purpose of this approach is for self-improvement, and often people will use it to relieve depression, stop smoking or find the inspiration they need to start a diet. Although some individuals can self-hypnotize, even others need help to achieve the altered state. To assist them in reaching that state, they can use hypnotic records or even mind machine machines. You should use self-hypnosis to improve your general physical well-being, calm, and overcome stage fright, among other things.

- **Stage Hypnosis**

The majority of people associate hypnosis with stage hypnosis. It is a type of entertainment in front of an audience in a theatre or a bar. The hypnotherapist is frequently depicted as a brilliant showman, which contributes to the perception that hypnosis is solely about mind control. The hypnotist would try to hypnotize the whole crowd at the start of the show before choosing a few people who fit the qualifications to come up on stage to perform various humiliating stunts, whereas the entire audience observes.

7.4. Neuro -Linguistic Programming

What comes to mind when you hear NLP? Isn't this anything coming out of Star Trek? You may be completely incorrect. The term "Neuron-linguistic programming" is a shorthand for "neuron-linguistic programming." It is one of the most common topics in the study of manipulation and dark psychology.

NLP has taken on many different interpretations over the years. It may be associated with the perception of adventure and excitement to learn more about the different forms of vaccinations that can affect many others as ourselves, providing us with a once-in-a-lifetime opportunity to improve ourselves or simply develop as individuals. It's also been described as a philosophy focused solely on the idea that all human behaviors have certain forms and mechanisms. These mechanisms and procedures can be repeated, instructed, learned, and modified.

It has also been described as a theme that has gradually developed into an advanced technology that helps us to manage our ideas and thoughts in ways that enable us to produce a series of outcomes that would otherwise be out of our control. The simplest and straightforward concept of NLP is that this is a learning mechanism that creates a specific language by creating associations between different senses of the body. It has been in use for over 40 years and has proven to be successful. NLP isn't as sealed off as you would imagine, but it's such a vast field with so many divisions and implementations that it's impossible to include all of them in our brief classification. If we are not comfortable with current behaviors, we will normally change or eliminate them, favoring a more appropriate collection of behaviors while we use this cryptic theme.

7.4.1. Types of Neuro-Linguistic Programming

Hypnotherapists have used a variety of NLP scripting techniques through the years. NLP Anchoring, NLP Flash, and NLP Reframe are three of the most common types of NLP.

a. NLP Anchoring

NLP Anchoring is the first form of NLP that will be addressed. Consider an old song you remember to get a better understanding of how anchoring works. Have you ever been driving and remembered a song you hadn't heard in a while? Did that song bring up a memory or a sensation from the past for you? You were going through these thoughts the first time you listened to that track, or later if you heard it, and your unconscious mind associated those feelings with that song. The song will be the anchor for such emotions as a result of this process. Now, any time you hear this tune, your brain will be triggered to get these emotions all over again. It is an excellent illustration of anchoring. Many hypnotists have discovered that anchoring is an effective method for hypnotizing their topics. The anchoring mechanism can inspire you to complete a task by associating pleasant thoughts with it. This approach, for example, is frequently used to make it easier to find the inspiration they need to adhere to a diet and lose weight. The hypnotist would collaborate with the target to establish an optimistic anchor consistent with the subject's mental image—in this case, the subject imagining themselves as slim and beautiful. When the subject sees this picture again, the anchor is triggered, and they receive the constructive reinforcement they need.

b. NLP Flash

NLP Flash is a type of hypnosis that is considered highly effective and can only be performed by a trained practitioner. It is frequently used to manipulate the subject's thoughts and emotions in their unconscious mind. It can be a useful tool for dealing with chronic depression or hooked to a drug. During this procedure, the hypnotist will turn the subject's emotions around. Instead of bringing joy, a certain act will begin to bring discomfort, or instead of bringing tension, the subject will experience relief. When someone is dependent on a drug like nicotine or alcohol, they will experience enjoyment and satisfaction when drinking the substance. These sensations can be turned around with the NLP flash technique, resulting in the person experiencing anxiety or pain as they ingest the drug. It will make it easier for them to overcome their addiction. Those under a lot of pressure have discovered that the NLP Flash strategy works effectively for them.

c. NLP Reframe

NLP Reframe is the third kind of NLP that has been employed in hypnosis. This approach is very powerful because it is so effective at aiding the target in changing their conduct. To carry out this procedure, the hypnotist must recognize that each person's actions result in a secondary reward or a beneficial outcome. The consequence of the actions is important because it explains the subject's action in response. Regardless of the significance of the result, the action used to achieve it is of secondary importance. During the reframe procedure, the hypnotist attempts to reason and bargain with the subject's unconscious mind. The objective is to encourage it to take over responsibility for adjusting to a new action accessible and successfully achieve the desired secondary benefit. Although all of this is going on in the amygdala, the subject's conscious mind will find the current action more rational. For example, suppose a person has a habit of eating to make themselves feel happier while they are depressed. In that case, the hypnotist can use this technique to persuade the unconscious to engage in different behavior. Exercise or reading a good book may be substituted for eating, allowing the subject to lose weight, eat healthily, and feel better overall.

7.5. Mechanism of Neuro-Linguistic Programming

Neuro-linguistic programming isn't normally focused on new-age mantras or the idea of hanging those medicinal trees in your room to get closer to your inner self. This dark psychology trend is generally based on a sound psychological theory. It is a brief mode of psychiatric counseling capable of solving a wide range of issues that we are destined to confront in our daily lives, including loneliness, phobias, and any bad behaviors we might have. In the long term, this is simply not an impulse toward an esoteric or spiritual solution to problems; using NLP would increase our success in both our professional and personal lives. Unlike conventional psychology, which relies on analyzing our situations to determine the root cause, NLP focuses on the infinite scenarios of how the brain functions to produce outcomes. As human beings, the ideas we have in our heads, the emotions we experience, and practically all we do are just what keeps us going. Changing these characteristics will lead to the appearance of a "different" you.

NLP is both a science and a kind of personal excellence. It's considered an art form for the simple reason that each individual has their distinct personality and way of doing things that can never be expressed in words or techniques. The science portion is due to the tool and procedure used to discover phenomena used by exceptional persons in every area to produce exceptional outcomes. The term "modeling" is another name for this procedure. Any trends and approaches found in this way have been seen more in the spheres of college, industry, athletics, and counseling over the years for more efficient engagement with everyone, a more comprehensive style of personal growth, and learning.

Have you ever tried incredibly hard on something just to be completely surprised by the result? Have you ever been surprised by something you did and wondering how you did as well as what you did it? NLP normally teaches you how to recognize and design your specific triumphs, helping you savor and multiply these euphoric feelings. It's a method of simply recognizing your true inner genius. Consider it a strategy for bringing out the best of yourself and those around you. It is a strategic ability that allows you to achieve the ultimate goals in the environment while also adding meaning to the lives of others. It analyzes what distinguishes the exceptional from the ordinary, leaving a trail of effective educational and business strategies in its wake. The three most critical aspects of shaping our human experience are commonly referred to as neuro-linguistic programming. The neural system governs how our bodies work, and language determines how we communicate and engage with people in our daily lives. Programming is a major component of all the representations and representations of the universe we build for ourselves. NLP aims to explain the overarching connection between the mind and words and their effect on our bodies and behavior when broken down. According to basic psyching, the self, the id, and the superego are the three central aspects of the psyche. Both models of developmental literature and experience appear to agree on these three points. Sees three models are present in NLP atoll, and it requires a more symbolic, extensible, and constructive approach. The NLP method advises that the innermost internal sections be undersold in a purely metaphorical context instead of a literal sense.

7.6. Different Types of Communications

Verbal and nonverbal communication are the two types of communication. Understanding all of them will help you get a deeper understanding of humans as a whole. To foster a strong base of information about connectivity, we ought to focus on them individually and explore the specifics. First, let's look at the visual conversation. Not only does having excellent listening skills make it easy for you all to comprehend others, but it also helps them understand you. While some people are natural communicators, others have a long way to go. Observing yourself in the mirror and engaging in certain contact exercises will make you realize how well you communicate with others around you. You may be shocked to learn that you have a lot of work ahead of you.

7.6.1. Verbal communications

The term "visual communication" refers to communication that takes place through the use of language. While this seems to be self-evident, did you even know that there have been four distinct forms of verbal communication? Most people don't pay attention to it, but it can make us understand what they are trying to say. Each method of verbal contact will provide us with information about ourselves and others.

7.6.2. Types of Verbal Communication

Let's discuss our types of verbal communication.

A. intrapersonal communication

Intrapersonal contact is the first kind. It is the internal dialogue we have with ourselves. We all spend lots of time in our heads chatting while trying to solve a tough dilemma or making a shopping list. Intrapersonal contact differs greatly between individuals. Some of us excel at putting ourselves together, while others rip ourselves apart in our words.

B. interpersonal communication

The interpersonal conversation is the next form of verbal

communication. It is the one-on-one talk you have with another human. Since one-on-one talks are more intimate, people can also take them very well. It tends to make you more insecure in comparison to being more intimate. That's because the conversation is solely between both of you.

C. Small-Group Communication

Then there's visual contact in small groups. More than two individuals participated in this, but the definition of a small party for verbal contact is unclear. It is a group of individuals who will all participate together in the dialogue. Consider topics like work squad sessions or news conferences. Everyone is taking turns to share their thoughts and opinions.

D. Public Communication

Public communication is the last form of verbal communication. There is usually only one speaker when talking about public relations. They'll be speaking to a wider audience. A prime example of this is election speeches. It's important to note so often and individuals behave in general than they would in person. Expecting a lot of improvements.

7.6.3. Non- Verbal Communication

Now it's time to consider nonverbal contact. Have you ever used the expression "it's not what you utter, nor how you say it"? It is important because, while what we say is significant, the nonverbal clues we send are even more. We spoke a lot about Neuro-Linguistic Programming earlier, and your nonverbal contact plays a big part in it. It's been reported that over 60% of just what we say is communicated by your body language rather than your actual speech. Understanding nonverbal contact will benefit you in several ways.

You'll get a better understanding of what people are trying to suggest. You will now be able to detect deception or lies more quickly. When you start paying attention to what a person's body is doing, you will figure out their real inspiration.

7.6.4. Types of non-verbal communication

There are so many types of non-verbal communication. Let's discuss a few of them.

a. Facial expressions

In nonverbal communication, observing someone's facial movements is a key indicator. Several lessons show us how to read facial expressions. Most of them are extremely easy. When you see someone laughing, it usually indicates that they are pleased or loving what they are doing. A grin, on the other hand, can be deceiving. Anxiety can be disguised as a smile. People who want to blend in but are unsure how can smile to be more open and friendly and less anxious. Tight lips can detect these smiles. You might even note that someone's smile seems to be artificial. You may be feeling this way. Going for the gut is a good example of this.

The more you pay attention to someone's voice, the more information you can glean from them. Ok, identifying a grin or a blush is easy, so what about the tiny, more difficult-to-detect expressions? Everyone's faces contain more than ten thousand different movement styles, and they all mean something, believe it or not. Learning more about the meanings of facial twitches and turns will assist you in identifying the rats within the crowd.

b. Body movements

Body movement, or kinesics, is also important in nonverbal communication. During talks, the movements reveal a lot of how we are feeling. Suppose we are involved in or concerned with what is being said. Paying enough attention to how people's bodies move can reveal a lot of their thoughts and feelings. Anybody's motions have a sense that we are familiar with. When we're having a chat, and someone looks at us and nods as we're talking, we know they're paying attention and listening to what we're saying. Some people might well be nodding but aren't paying attention. It can be seen in their eye movement. It may be due to boredom or obsessive thought. Someone that clears their throat is probably embarrassed over what they're saying, but they may still be attempting to catch someone's attention which is disturbed.

Nervous ticks are often found in people who are about to do something illegal or dangerous to others. When you do something wrong, you are likely to feel some form of remorse because you have deep Dark Triad characteristics. As the body rejects the act about to be executed, this will refer to body movement clues.

c. Eye contact

Face contact is another important aspect of nonverbal communication. Maintaining eye contact can be tough for some people. It might make you feel like they aren't paying attention or are Shifty. It's none of this stuff for others. They find it unsettling to look someone in the eyes when conversing. Maintaining eye contact with someone you're speaking with demonstrates that you're involved and active in what they're doing. It does not imply that you would gaze them down the whole time they are speaking. Frequent eye contact, on the other hand, will significantly increase communication. Experts also discovered that staring someone in the eyes while still looking at their other attributes will make you feel more at ease. It might be less painful if you shift your gaze to their eyelids, nose, and other parts of their profile. Of course, you'll still want to glance them inside the eyes when they're chatting. People who have committed or want to commit offenses have a difficult time keeping in touch. The eyes have been said to be the window to the soul, and there is some merit to this. When you pay attention to how someone's eyes turn and look, you will figure out whether they have good or evil intentions.

d. Paralanguage

Nonverbal contact includes paralanguage. It covers a variety of topics that can enable you to connect more effectively. Tone, tempo, and inflection are the three major components. All of these components are essential in understanding what you're saying. In nonverbal communication, the sound of the voice is also very important. It can entice or repel listeners. A monotone voice lacks inflection. Each term is spoken with the same tone and pace. A monotone speaker's cadence is gradual and consistent in their sentences. It can be difficult to listen to this. Changing your tone while speaking with others will make them understand what you will be feeling. We can communicate our feelings in the sound of our words, which makes for easier contact. When it comes to public speaking, using a great sound will get you far.

Voice inflection is equally significant, as they all play an important role in successful verbal communication. A piece of nonverbal correspondence is part communication. What else do we think about if we want to develop our nonverbal communication skills? It is a difficult question to answer because nonverbal contact involves too many. We may glance at the top of an iceberg for a moment, but nonverbal contact is something that people research for years.

7.7. Improvement in body language

One of the most telling indicators of how someone is feeling and what they might be planning is their body language. The way a person acts and reacts during a meeting, out in public, and at home reveals a lot of what's going on with them at the time. Many who are practicing NLP methods devote a significant amount of time to researching body language. Body language is what we communicate without doing something. It can indicate whether you're happy, depressed, open to discussion, or shut off from the rest of the world. It is visible not only through the physical body as well as through your eyes. NLP further emphasizes paying close attention to the eyes. Any realities could be contained in body language, which isn't always reflected in the words that come out of someone's mouth.

According to research, we can learn more about a person from their facial gestures, pupils, and body language as we can from their spoken words. As a result, learning to recognize body language will benefit you in almost any situation. Seeing how shady people behave will assist you in mitigating problems.

You will be able to recognize certain feelings when you first start talking about body language. We all understand what a person's face looks like, whether they're excited or sad. The symptoms are easy to see, but determining whether someone is nervous or depressed can be more difficult.

Nonverbal signals will lead you to some part of your body. Slightly dilated eyes, for example, may not be due to a blinding light but rather to arousal. It may be a symptom of stalling or increased discomfort in the present situation if someone is continually chewing their lower lip.

The way a person stands or sits may also provide information about how they are feeling. When someone's arms are folded around them, they are much less inclined to want to be confronted. A relaxed posture with your arms on your hips, on the other hand, indicates that you are probably in command of the scenario or that you are threatening.

These kinds of skills will significantly increase the ability to spot a weirdo in a crowd.

If you have been in a place and seen someone behaving strangely, this is about you. You know, like running around the room a lot and not maintaining eye contact during conversations. Since most individuals have at least a rudimentary understanding of how to decipher a person's body language, you'll be able to spot these.

What the body is signaling to other people is often influenced by your stance. People that sit up and tie their hands around themselves are known to be locked off.

They might be becoming uncomfortable or worried. A relaxed stance with the heads high and shoulders down, on the other hand, is very inviting. It demonstrates that you are approachable, polite, and receptive to discussion.

Neither your body language influence how people approach you, but it also influences how you view others. When it comes to body language, there are several factors to remember. The more you learn about NLP, the more body language you can notice. It may be veryuseful in identifying people who are dangerous and maybe acting maliciously.

Chapter 8. The Technique of Brainwashing

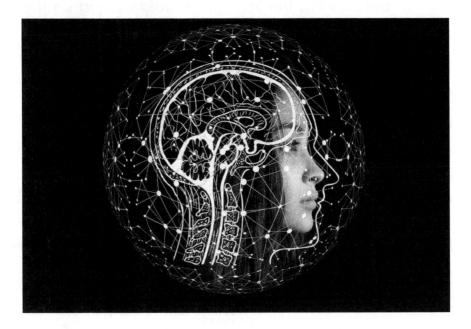

The application of brainwashing in psychology will be explored in this book. Brainwashing is described as a process of thought change by social influence in this context. Every individual is subjected to this type of social impact daily, whether they are aware of it or not. The term "social control" refers to a collection of techniques for influencing other people's habits, values, and attitudes.

8.1. Definition of Brainwashing

Most psychologists believe that if the right circumstances are present, it is feasible to brainwash a subject. And then, the entire thing isn't almost as bad as it seems in the papers. There are also several meanings of brainwashing, making determining the impact of brainwashing on the topic more complex. Some of these meanings stipulate that the subject's physical body must be threatened somehow to be called brainwashing. If this idea were followed, then the activities of certain radical cults will not be called actual brainwashing when no physical violence is involved. Most concepts of brainwashing would depend on control and manipulation without the use of physical action to alter the subjects' views.

In either case, psychologists agree that the effects of brainwashing are only temporary, particularly in optimal circumstances. They assume that the practice does not entirely erase the subject's old identity; rather, it is hidden and can resurface until the current identity is no longer reinforced.

8.2. Steps of Brainwashing

Modern psychology divides brainwashing into three stages to help explain what happens to the subject during the process. The deconstructing of the self, the introduction of the concept of redemption to the subject, and the restoration of the subject's self are the three steps. Understanding each of these steps and the processes that occur during each of them will help you understand what is happening in the subject's personality during this period.

1. Self-Destructive Behavior

The breakdown of the self is the first step of the brainwashing process. The agent needs to shatter the subject's old identity during this phase in making people feel more insecure and vulnerable to the ideal new identity. This move is needed to proceed with the procedure. If the topic is still deeply fixed in their determination and their old identity, the agent will not be very good in their efforts. Breaking up that identification and letting the individual doubt their surroundings will make changing the identity simpler in the future. It is accomplished by a series of steps that include assassinating the subject's identity, instilling remorse, self-betrayal, and finally hitting the breaking point.

i.   Assault on Identity

The systemic attack on the subject's sense of self, ego, or personality and their central conviction system is an assault on the subject's identity.

ii.   Guilt

The subject would reach the stage of remorse after they have survived the attack on their identity. As the subject is going through this current identity struggle, the subject will be repeatedly convinced that victims are evil.

iii.   Self-betrayal

The agent will force the target to accept that they are bad now that they have been led to think that they have been worse and that all of their acts are unacceptable. The victim is sinking in their shame and feels very disoriented at this stage.

iv.   Breaking Point

The subject is completely exhausted and disoriented at this stage. The subject might inquire, "Where am I?" or "What am I doing?" What do I do if I'm not sure who I am? At this moment, the subject is having an identity crisis and is experiencing profound guilt.

2. Possibility of Salvation

It's time to go onto another level after the negotiator has successfully broken down the subject's self. This move entails giving the subject the hope of redemption only if they can abandon their previous belief system in favor of the presented one. The topic is allowed to comprehend what is going on around them, and they are assured that if they only take the new ideal direction, they will be successful again and feel better. This step of the brainwashing method includes four steps: leniency, desire to confess, channeling of remorse, and guilt release.

i.   Leniency

The stage of leniency is where you say, "I will support you." The topic has been deconstructed and made to step back from the person and the values they have maintained for so long. They've been told that they're poor people who do something wrong.

ii.   Compulsion to Confession

If the agent has gained the confidence of their target, they may attempt to extract a confession from them. This period is often referred to as the "You can support yourself" stage. The subject begins to see the inconsistencies between the discomfort and remorse they faced during the personality attack and their comfort from the unexpected leniency provided throughout that stage of the brainwashing operation.

iii.   Guilt Channeling

The subject has been enduring the attack on themselves for several months by the time they reach the channel of guilt. The subject will sense the remorse and embarrassment that has been placed on them by the time they hit this stage in the brainwashing process, but it has lost much of its significance.

iv.   Releasing of Guilt

The subject has realized that their old ideals and beliefs are causing them pain in this phase. They are worn down and weary of the blame and stigma imposed on themselves for many years.

3. Self-Reconstruction

The topic has been through several measures and emotional stress by this point. They've been placed through an experience designed to rob them of their previous selves, convinced that they're poor and ought to be repaired, and have gradually realized that their value structure is the source of their wrongdoing and that it has to be modified. After everything has been accomplished, the subject will have to practice how to reconstruct themselves with the agent's assistance.

Since the topic is a blank canvas and ready to practice about being and feel healthier, this stage gives the agent the ability to implant the new system's ideas. There are two stages to be seen during this point: harmony and the final confession until starting over.

i.   Harmony

The agent would use this move to persuade the subject that making a transition is their decision. They should remind the topic that they may have the power to do what is right for them and make a difference that would make them feel better.

ii.   Final Confession and a New Beginning

About the fact that the decision isn't theirs, the negotiator has worked hard the entire time to make the subject believe they have the freedom to choose another identity. If the brainwashing procedure is performed right, the target will consider the new options objectively and decide that adopting the new persona is the better option.

8.3. Techniques of Brainwashing

Brainwashing techniques are employed in a variety of ways. The intensity of brainwashing mentioned in this section is not always the case. The techniques mentioned are only used for "true brainwashing" and are seldom used. Several other forms of brainwashing exist daily.

They do not force you to leave your old persona searching for a particular one, but they do assist you in shifting your perspective on what is happening around you. This segment will look at some of the commonly used techniques throughout the brainwashing operation, whether real or not.

- **Hypnosis**

Hypnosis can be used to brainwash people. Hypnosis, in general, causes a high level of suggestibility. It is often covered up as sleep or relaxing. During hypnosis, the agent will make suggestions to the subject in the hopes that they will respond or behave in any way.

- **Love Bombing**

People have a deep sense of belonging to their families. It is the party into which you have been born and with which you have supposedly spent your whole life. You know more than anybody, and those who have missed out on such a relationship can feel alone and unwelcome. Through love bombing, the manipulator will build a sense of family through emotional attachment, feeling and sharing, and physical contact. It creates a family bond between the trickster and the subject, making it much easier to swap in the old one's old identity.

- **Unbending rules**

The manipulator's laws are always rigid and

unchangeable. These laws make it impossible for the survivor to look and behave independently; instead, they will waste their time doing just as the manipulator says. This division encompasses a wide range of laws, from those governing disorientation and relapse to those governing the use of medications, bathroom breaks, and food. These guidelines are to monitor the victim through the brainwashing process fully.

- **Verbal abuse**

Most of the strategies employed during the divorce process are verbal assault. When a survivor is continuously bombarded with violent and coarse words, he or she sometimes becomes desensitized. Physical harassment may also be used in addition to or instead of verbal abuse.

- **Controlled approval**

During the break-up time, the manipulator can work to retain doubt and weakness. Regulated acceptance is one method of accomplishing this. In exchange, the manipulator can threaten and recompense reciprocal acts, making it impossible for the survivor to decide what is right and wrong.

- **Rejecting old values**

As discussed earlier in this segment, the manipulator attempts to convince the target to abandon all of his beliefs. This phase is accelerated by intimidation, physical attacks, and other methods. Finally, the target will abandon its previous ideals and convictions and continue to embrace the manipulator's traditional way of living.

- **Confusing Doctrine**

This strategy would allow the survivor to embrace the new identification without question while dismissing all other logic he or she might have. To ensure that, the manipulator is subjected to a series of convoluted lessons on an incomprehensible principle. The subject will start to tolerate whatever the agent suggests, whether it be about the ideology or a new start formed, through this mechanism.

- **Metacommunication**

When the manipulator sends subliminal signals to the victim, this technique is used. When the agent stresses those words or phrases critical to the current persona, this is achieved. The terms and keywords are inserted into long, confusing lectures that the subject is expected to sit through.

- **No Privacy**

Many victims would forfeit their right to privacy until they have assumed a new identity. It is done not only to make the victim's remorse and wrongdoings more apparent, but it also takes away the subject's capacity to evaluate what is said objectively. If the target has anonymity, they may have time to consider the private information and discover that they are lying or not living up to expectations. Through removing this anonymity, the investigator or cop will be there at all times and will still direct the subject to a different identification.

- **Disinhibition**

During this technique, the manipulator urges the victim to obey like a puppy. It makes it easier for the manipulator to shape the subject's mind.

- **The change in diet**

Changing the victim's diet is another technique that causes restlessness while increasing the subject's vulnerability to emotional excitement. When the manipulator greatly decreases the amount of food the victim can eat, the victim's nervous system is robbed of the carbohydrates it requires to thrive. Drugs may be thrown into the mix in this group.

- **Games**

Games are often used to instill a stronger sense of collective cohesion. Games will be added, and completely enigmatic laws could plague the majority of them. The subject is not always informed of the law, which must be known, or the rules are continuously changing. This strategy allows the agent to exert more leverage.

- **No question**

During the brainwashing process, the survivor is not able to ask any questions. Issues encourage independent thought, which is hazardous for brainwashing. If no queries are raised, the agent is more likely to recognize the victim's new identification on the spot.

- **Guilt**

The survivor was advised that they are evil and that they just do bad things. The manipulator also employs guilt to challenge their convictions and the events that occur around them. The abuses of the victim's previous lifestyle are exaggerated to add guilt to live and increase the victim's desire for redemption.

- **Fear**

Fear is an effective motivator that can accomplish even

better than the other strategies. Manipulators can use fear to keep the group's desired obedience and allegiance. To accomplish this, the manipulator will risk the individual's life, limb, or soul if they oppose the new persona in any way.

- **Deprivation of sleep**

Sleep deprivation is a condition in which a person is deprived of sleep

You will also be vulnerable and disoriented if you do not get enough sleep. It will assist in creating the desired atmosphere that the manipulator needs during the breakdown and denomination of the brainwashing operation. Furthermore, victims are often forced to engage in prolonged physical and emotional exercises and sleep deprivation to hasten the process.

- **Dress codes**

Implementing a dress code merely diminishes the victim's individuality and his ability to choose his clothing. During the brainwashing process, the survivor is often asked to follow the group's dress code.

- **Confession**

Confession is highly promoted among people who are

transitioning through their previous life to their current identity. By recognizing the agent's innermost fears and personal shortcomings, the subject loses its internal ego during this period. The new persona can be adopted after you've moved past this stuff.

- **Financial commitments**

In certain circumstances, financial donations are expected. It will assist the officer in a variety of areas. The financial contribution allows the subject to lean more heavily on the community because they could be burning bridges with their history. They donate various things, such as their car, house, property, or other financial donation, in the hopes of overcoming their shame and remorse. They are now financially tied to the current persona. Furthermore, the agent can use these financial donations to support its own needs.

- **Chanting**

the agent attempts to rid the victim's mind of any uncultured ideas. Chanting or repeating words used by those who adopt the current identity is one way to do this.

- **Pointing your finger**

You can feel righteous if you can raise a finger at someone else. It is the way of demonstrating to the universe that you are fine by pointing out some of the world's flaws. The manipulator can point out all of the world's murder, bigotry, and chasms before comparing them with the good of the victim's new identity.

- **Isolation**

It's difficult to have outside feedback that could persuade you to change your mind while you're cut off from the rest of the world. Since subjects wouldn't need to get free with all their jobs, the agent will do this. The brainwashers would be cut off from civilization, their peers, and their relatives, as well as all other logical sources that could influence their reasoning.

8.4. Prevention from Brainwashing

Here are four ways to stop being brainwashed in your personal or professional life:

- **Recognize yourself**

We don't take the opportunity to meet ourselves well enough all too much. Spend some time considering your belief structure, who and what you are, where your Region of Genius is, and what is and is not important to you. It's quick to be persuaded into a path that isn't good for us if we don't have this. For example, perhaps your parents instilled in you the desire to be a doctor. However, if you don't understand what it takes to be a successful doctor and how your talents compare, you may do it blindly only to discover later that it isn't the right career for you.

The more effectively the message is delivered, the more inclined you are to adopt it. When you enter society, a career, or a school, consider whether the community reflects who and what you are, lifeblood.

- **Have a definite vision for the future and career**

When you have a clear vision, it's difficult to stray from it. If you don't have a clear vision, you're more likely to be fooled by unconventional solutions or inspiring figures. Take the time to create a vision and refresh it to ensure that it is the best one when you are at each stage of your life.

- **To ponder and to be inquisitive**

Most of the time, we don't give our lives much thought. We wait before something goes wrong before we come to the realization and something needs to change. Instead of putting things aside, begin to make it a habit to reflect on your life and work. Use your imagination to venture beyond the window, whether it's to solve a dilemma or go on a new journey in life.

- **Be open while being grounded**

Being transparent means admitting that you don't understand anything, which is a wonderful thing. Discover new information and remain grounded in your approach to assimilating it. Do any reading, read a book, watch a movie, or look for facts in such a way that interests you. Concentrate on the topics that fascinate you. If you're especially persuaded by something or someone, take that as a hint that you need to learn more about it. When sifting through data, look past the obvious.

The fact of the matter is that it's all too tempting to get complacent in being loyal to oneself and putting in the effort required to avoid getting brainwashed by others. It's in our nature to want to fit in, so the sooner we identify with others around us, the better likely we will be accepted into the community. The trick is to be mindful of it either before or after the event. Make an effort to reconnect with yourself. It would be much more difficult for someone to persuade you to have been someone you are not if you do this.

Click here if you want to know the TEN STRATEGIC AND POWERFUL SALES PERSUASION TECHNIQUES for Free →
http://bit.ly/10strategic

Conclusion

Thank you for reading Dark Psychology And Manipulation: The Powerful Strategic Techniques of Dark Psychology and Manipulation, Brainwashing, NLP, Persuasion, and Hypnosis to the end. I hope you've learned how manipulators operate and how to protect yourself against them so you can reclaim ownership of your life.

The next move is to become more vigilant in your dealings with manipulators and those with dark personality characteristics. Don't let yourself become a survivor. Instead, you can use what you've learned here to observe the people you communicate with within a family, at the workplace, and in social situations so that you can appreciate what they're up to. Don't let evil people take you off guard now that you've learned your lesson.

It's time to bring an end to family and friends or any other person of the life who has been exploiting you regularly. Use the strategies we've covered to fight back against those attempting to take control of your life.

Now that you've read " Dark Psychology And Manipulation: The Powerful Strategic Techniques of Dark Psychology and Manipulation, Brainwashing, NLP, Persuasion, and Hypnosis," we think it's important to emphasize that you have to protect the people in your life. Do anything if you suspect that anyone you care for is being abused or victimized. Often, don't use your abilities for evil, and don't use these tactics to harm others.

If you enjoyed this book, please let me know your thoughts by leaving a short review on Amazon.

Thank you so much!

CPSIA information can be obtained
at www.ICGtesting.com
Printed in the USA
LVHW052243060721
692003LV00011B/1255